BILLY MITCHELL

LIVES TO REMEMBER

Billy Mitchell

America's Eagle of Air Power

by Arch Whitehouse

G. P. PUTNAM'S SONS
NEW YORK

© 1962 by Arch Whitehouse

All rights reserved

Library of Congress Catalog
Card Number: 61-8035

MANUFACTURED IN THE UNITED STATES OF AMERICA

VAN REES PRESS • NEW YORK

Published simultaneously in the Dominion of Canada by
Longmans, Green and Company, Toronto

CONTENTS

Dedicated to

The Air-Minded Youth of America

INTRODUCTION

The story of General William E. Mitchell is more than the history of an American military hero. His career presents a lesson for the people of our nation. It offers high adventure, heroism, leadership and attainment. Billy Mitchell, as the saying goes, "did everything," and few of our battlefield heroes can compare with him.

Although he came from a family of wealth and social standing, Mitchell was probably the most democratic figure in modern military history. He began his service by enlisting as a private. What rank he attained he earned in the field. He combined leadership with personal example to an extent that no present-day hero has attained. He asked for and received no favors. He was awarded a dozen decorations for valor, and his courage was recognized by our Allies as well as by his own government.

For years he was the Wonder Man of the American Army and if this book had been offered as a standard-hero story, Mitchell would have filled the bill with plenty to spare; but we all have to learn that life—in or out of the services—is not a chapter of heroics and awards. There are setbacks, tragedies, frustrations and mistakes in all phases of human endeavor. Billy Mitchell had more than his share. He might have bowed out and ended his career on a golden note of accomplishment, but as he explained later, he had to live with his conscience. As a result he died, his record tarnished by the verdict of an unrealistic court-martial; simply because he was determined to build a sound air defense for his country.

He was misunderstood, ignored, rebuffed and discarded. He was not always right, but he believed he was, and perhaps his burning patriotism often tempered his views and decisions. That he died with the stigma of a court-martial verdict against him, should be a lesson for everyone, for it teaches us that life does not always respond to man's hopes and aspirations.

Billy Mitchell represented a period of time that to some extent has been forgotten. He was born in December 1879 (practically 1880) and lived until 1936—a little more than half a century. But what a half century he encompassed! In that time he had seen and experienced many of the major influences of our present-day civilization. He took part in the Cuban uprising, fought in the Philippines, observed the early Balkan wars, and played a major part in World War I as an aviator. This in itself puts him in a very special category. Although he was not an "ace," with many planes to his credit, his service was brightly reflected in America's part in that conflict.

Mitchell was an important figure in the era that saw

the full development of the machine gun, modern artillery, trench warfare, the use of poison gas, flamethrowers, armored tanks and the fledgling efforts of wartime aviators. Thus he was something of a military pioneer. His period of history, the early Twentieth Century, has so recently passed that it has been carelessly tossed aside and to some extent ignored. Yet this half century produced more great events and inventions than all previous history combined. It gave us radio, television, underseas cables, the airplane, transoceanic flying, multimessage telephone systems, the internal-combustion engine, the submarine, the beginning of the jet age and motion pictures. It saw great strides in international business and commerce. Geography changed and many reigning monarchs toppled. Sports records and speed marks increased and the phrase "a mile a minute" no longer impressed anyone. Great explorations were completed, mountain peaks conquered, and a new breed of man was developed. Billy Mitchell was a leader of this bold company.

A fantastic tapestry of history, then, is the backdrop for General Billy Mitchell's stormy career. We have almost everything to work with, for he was an important figure in that history. He served long and well, and his tragic efforts to build a unified Air Service along strategic lines were not fully understood or appreciated until our country found itself once more entangled in a global war.

Arch Whitehouse

October 29, 1961

BILLY MITCHELL

LIVES TO REMEMBER

Chapter 1

KNIGHT OF THE AIR

The sleek, bulldog-type Spad fighter had been ranging up and down the Western Front for more than an hour. The pilot, a keen-eyed, compactly knit man, was keeping a sharp lookout ahead, above and below. He stayed clear of air action or combat for he was seeking information; not personal glory. He watched the various formations as they moved into attack positions. He pondered on the tactics employed and made short, critical notes on a block fastened to a small board near his elbow.

Now and then he would move in closer, mainly to give some moral support to a few two-seaters spotting for American artillery, or churning through the deadly chore of gathering strips of photographs for infantry intelligence. He provided aid where it was necessary, but his chief concern was to find an answer to a dozen important questions.

The pilot was Colonel William E. Mitchell, Chief of America's Air Service in France. With such responsibility he had little excuse for exposing himself to the enemy in this manner, but he had long realized that if there was anything he wished to know, finding it out in his own way was the most satisfactory.

Billy Mitchell was accountable for all the American active-service squadrons on the front, a job that required considerable desk- and paperwork, but the men closely associated with him were not flyers and could not answer many of his questions. So several days a week Colonel Mitchell took off to discover the answers for himself.

World War I had been stalemated for more than four years. Neither side could claim any outstanding victory; only grim losses and setbacks had been suffered. As Billy Mitchell churned up and down the lines, he sought the reason for this standoff. A hundred other high-ranking officials on both sides had searched for the same solution, but so far there had been no answer to this military enigma. How to win the war had plagued many minds.

Below were the irregular tracings of the trenches. In front and to the rear were the white festers of shell-fire. Those zigzagging lines were the communication trenches through which men relieved other men every few days. Where one could see short, straight ditches with round depressions at one end, there were small groups of men huddled around machine guns protected by low barriers of sandbags. This was the pattern of trench warfare. In these deep slots, crouching from the artillery, mortar fire and the choking fumes of poison gas, men had fought and held on for four long years.

The trenches were marked in another manner too. Every few miles, on both sides of the lines, Colonel Mitchell could see large, bulbous kite balloons swinging from steel cables. In the baskets slung beneath them, skilled observers watched the ground activities of their enemies, and what they saw was telephoned down the same cable to men on the ground who in turn relayed the information to those most concerned.

Billy Mitchell had long realized that never before in all history had such a war been conceived and fought. Never before had such weapons been employed. Never before had so many men fought so long for practically no advantage. What was the answer to the dreadful stalemate? By now nearly 8,000,000 men had been killed on both sides and more than 20,000,000 had been wounded. Seven million more were either missing or prisoners of war. The total casualties up until September 1918 had reached the unbelievable figure of 37,000,000.

Colonel Mitchell had searched for an answer on every front, with every Allied service and from behind practically every type of weapon. He knew the whiplash effect of the machine gun, the crushing impact of heavy artillery. He had seen men cut down by poison gas or seared to death by flame-throwers. He had huddled in a front-line trench and watched behemoth tanks trundle across no man's land in the hope of breaking up the entrenched stalemate, but so far they had proven to be only armored cavalry. They could move about and drive infantrymen out of shallow redoubts and tear out barbed wire entanglements so that their own infantry might advance a few yards, but they could do little to produce a final decision.

Billy Mitchell had high hopes for the airplane. He had seen dogfights at high altitudes, where men shot down other men. He had seen attack planes sweep over enemy trenches, spraying infantrymen with machine-gun fire, or breaking down emplacements with light bombs. He had been on long-distance bombing raids that were aimed to break up large concentrations and important railroad centers, or destroy enemy-supply dumps. All very dramatic, and at times romantic, but none of it provided the answer to finishing the War.

"We are going about this in the wrong way," Billy said, as he had many times before. "We're missing something important. We are wasting our efforts, our equipment and our manpower. There must be an answer to this, somewhere."

He turned away from the enemy antiaircraft fire, watched a desultory combat between a small formation of Fokkers and Allied Nieuports, and then made his way back to Toul to his headquarters. He put down the Spad gently, released his safety belt, and hauled himself wearily from his cockpit.

"You are wanted on the telephone, sir," Mitchell's orderly announced when Billy strode into his office.

"Who is it?"

"Major Harold H. Hartney, Commander First Pursuit Group, sir."

"Oh yes. Giving his daily report on air fighting."

"Not exactly, sir. Will you take it in your cubicle?"

"Be right there." Billy tossed his flight gear to the orderly.

He picked up the field phone and said, "Hello, Harold. What's on your mind?"

"Good afternoon, sir. Do you have a few minutes later on, to watch a special front-line show?"

"Who's putting it on?"

"That kid Luke. Frank Luke."

"Don't tell me he's still with you," Colonel Mitchell responded with a grin. "What's he up to now?"

"He and Joe Wehner have promised to knock down three kite balloons . . . one, two, three . . . just like that."

Colonel Mitchell frowned and broke in, "What do they think this War is—a game? Just what is the idea?"

Hartney tried to explain: "They're making it a sort of game, I suppose. Anyway, Luke says he'll shoot down the first at seven-ten, the second at seven-twenty and the third at seven-thirty. The boys are making bets on it."

"Wehner is tailing him?"

"That's right, sir. Those two are thicker than thieves."

"A very apt phrase, Major. I'll run over and see if they get away with it."

Colonel Mitchell had little enthusiasm for this kite-balloon business, particularly when it was run on such happy-go-lucky lines. He turned toward the progress charts on his office wall. He should have been satisfied with the graphs and figures there, for considering what he had to work with and the hand-me-down aircraft that had been furnished by the French and British, his front-line squadrons were doing very well. He had a number of high-scoring aces, his artillery-co-operating plane crews were learning fast, and his bomber squadrons were delivering their share of high explosive on enemy-held positions. Actually, his United States Air Service in the field was getting into high gear, and had accomplished much of which Mitchell could be proud.

But the colonel was far from satisfied. He had been an American observer on the Western Front before his country had joined the Allies. He was a newcomer to aviation but he had carefully studied the methods used by the French and British and learned a great deal. More important, he had won the friendship of General Hugh "Boom" Trenchard, former Commander in Chief of the Royal Flying Corps. Like Mitchell, Trenchard was a forthright man with unorthodox views concerning the use of military aircraft; views that gradually had been forming in Billy Mitchell's mind.

It was their combined opinion that the highly publicized aces, the glamorous airmen who were running up high scores and gaining all the decorations, were not earning their keep. Perhaps it would be better to say that they were being misused. This Mitchell-Trenchard viewpoint ran contrary to popular opinion, for many people measured the progress of the war in the victory scores of the headliners of that day. They had thrilled to the records of Charles Nungesser, Jimmy McCudden, Baron von Richthofen, Albert Ball, Georges Guynemer, Werner Voss, Billy Bishop, René Fonck and Oswald Boelcke. Now the American stars—Raoul Lufbery, Eddie Rickenbacker, Douglas Campbell, David Putnam and Elliott White Springs were making the headlines. All of these performers had shot down hundreds of opposition aircraft. What did Mitchell and Trenchard mean when they said the aces were not paying their way?

Billy Mitchell had an idea—so far it had not completely jelled—that the warplane was being improperly employed. Perhaps it was given the wrong tasks. Mitchell, who was to become the stormy petrel of American military aviation, was soon to discover what the solution entailed.

Colonel Mitchell had a kindred spirit over at Number 27 Squadron, based at Saintes, a short distance from the U. S. Air Service Headquarters. On this evening in question Second Lieutenant Frank Luke had made the boast that he would destroy three enemy kite balloons within twenty minutes.

Most pilots of that era were content with one victory a day, and most of them preferred to fight enemy aircraft—not kite balloons. Observation *drachens,* to give them their original name, were very risky targets. They were highly important to the German Intelligence Staff, and every precaution was taken to keep them in the air, since they afforded valuable information over critical battle areas for many consecutive hours a day.

These kite balloons, which were tethered to a motor-driven winch on the ground, could be raised to levels between 3,000 and 5,000 feet, and telephonic communication was available at all times from the observers in the baskets. They were always well guarded by batteries of antiaircraft guns and regular patrols of fighter planes.

To add to the danger of attacking these balloons, one in four or five was sent aloft with dummy observers in the basket and several hundred pounds of high explosive in canisters. These "booby traps" could be detonated from the ground, or they might explode with widespread destruction when an enemy fighter or aerial gunner poured a burst of bullets into the basket. There were several tricks of this sort to be played by the men responsible for the maintenance of the balloon line.

Frank Luke was the "Peck's Bad Boy" of the American Air Service. A chip-on-the-shoulder, undisciplined Arizonan, he had given his superiors and squadron companions a bad time from the day he joined Number 27 Squadron. Lieutenant Joe Wehner was the only pilot in the squadron with whom Luke would associate. Joe, too, was something of an outcast, but for different reasons. Although born in Massachusetts, Joe had a Teutonic name and was continually under unfounded suspicion. He had been investigated by government officials ever since volunteering, but Joe Wehner was as true blue an American as any flyer in the group.

The two balloon busters took off shortly after dinner and the rest of the squadron turned out to watch the fun. There were a few cynics in the group who could not resist viewing the exploit. The enemy balloon line was about ten miles from the Saintes field, but the gasbags could be seen plainly with binoculars in fair weather. If they were attacked successfully, they would go up like great bonfires in the oncoming darkness.

Major Hartney and Captain Alfred Grant, Commander of Number 27 Squadron, stood together in the cool night air and waited. A few miles away Colonel Mitchell was roaring along a French road in a huge Mercedes touring car. At exactly 7:10 P.M. the first balloon went up; a great scarlet blossom against the deepening sky. Luke was one minute late on the second. It did not blaze up until 7:21, but was a thriller when it exploded. Waiting for the third balloon left everyone limp and considerably concerned. Major Hartney was chain smoking and Captain Grant was tramping up and down, regretting that he had sanctioned this dangerous exploit. Neither noticed Colonel Mitchell's blunderbuss Mercedes as it roared around the hangars.

"Come on, Luke! Come on, kid!"

Up forward, beyond the American trenches, two roaring Spads were darting about, trying to disguise their next moves. After the first two kites had been shot down, it was quite possible that the ground crews in the area would haul down the third, so Luke and Wehner curled away and returned to their own back area for a few minutes. They cruised up and down, faking a line patrol, until Joe was positive that Number 3 was still aloft.

There was no inter-plane communication in those days and they had to fly wing tip to wing tip and use exaggerated gestures. Finally Luke saw the balloon too, and with a wild wing over he led the way back through the wicked barrage of antiaircraft fire coming up from the trenches, the back areas and the batteries assigned to protect the kites.

"It was the worst we ever encountered," Joe explained later. "Just like flying through a hailstorm of old nuts and bolts."

Luke ignored the shrapnel curtain and continued to race at the *drachen*. He pulled up his hydraulic-interrupter gear handle and made sure both guns were properly synchronized.

Back at the Saintes field someone was tolling off the minutes, staring at a wrist watch: "It is now seven-thirty-one . . . seven-thirty-two . . . seven-thirty-three . . . seven-thirty-four . . ."

"How's he doing?" Colonel Mitchell whispered into Major Hartney's ear. The major jumped as though he had been prodded with a bayonet.

"Hi . . . Hello, Colonel. He's O.K. so far. Two of them went up on time, but it is now seven-thirty-six. Something must have happened."

"Give him time. I know what it's like up there."

Suddenly the sky took on a rosy glow, as though someone had lifted a giant stove lid in a dark kitchen. Number 3 had been torched, just as Frank Luke had promised.

Both Mitchell and Hartney breathed deep sighs of relief.

"Now we have to get them back," the colonel said, peering up into the enveloping gloom.

"I planned to set up a row of fires to mark the landing area," Major Hartney explained.

"Give everyone a Very pistol and a pocketful of signal flares," Mitchell ordered. "We'll get those kids back if we have to illuminate all France."

While they waited for Luke and Wehner to return, the colonel pondered on the amazing performance of these two pilots. Although they had destroyed three enemy kite balloons, he wondered whether the combined risk was worth it. He walked away from the jubilant group and sat down in the front seat of his car.

Those balloons should never have been there in the first place, he mused. They should never have been completed at some German balloon factory. For that matter, the rubber used in the fabric shouldn't have reached Germany at all. And what about the cokeworks that produced the gas to inflate them? But all these factors were brought together and the balloons were shipped to the front, inflated, and run up from expensive winch equipment. If we had staged a careful bomb strike we could have at least destroyed the balloon factory. We could have blown up the gas-producing plants. In that case there wouldn't have been a balloon up anywhere along the front. General Trenchard is right.

Luke and Wehner returned safely and put down their Spads amid a wild greeting and a fireworks display that would have shamed a World's Fair. While Major Hartney and Captain Grant took the two balloon busters back to the mess for a real celebration Colonel Mitchell remained out on the field alone. By now he was figuring out how more practical illumination could be devised to make conditions safer for these kids who wanted to fly day and night, Sundays and holidays.

Their success was as heady as wine, and both Luke and Wehner believed that they could keep this up day after day. Mitchell and Hartney knew that the law of averages would eventually take its toll. However, they were wise enough not to make it seem that they were trying to hogtie the courage of these young men.

Two days after the three-balloon show Joe Wehner "went west" during another wild foray against the enemy kites. While protecting Luke's tail he was shot down by half a dozen Fokkers which had darted in when Joe was intent on staying with Frank.

Luke, now known as the Arizona Balloon Buster, was inconsolable, and Major Hartney decided that a change of scene was needed. He conspired with Colonel

Mitchell to have Frank sent to Paris for a fourteen-day furlough. He even drove Frank to the nearest railhead to make sure the Arizonan got aboard the train.

Less than a week later Luke returned, still morose and silent.

Major Hartney roared over from First Pursuit Headquarters and demanded to know why Luke was back so early.

"There wasn't anything to do," Frank explained, and really meant every word of it. The gayest wartime city in the world had nothing to offer—there were no enemy balloons to destroy over Paris.

Colonel Mitchell and Major Hartney accepted the inevitable, and Frank Luke went back to combat flying. After he had set up another three-balloon show and had shot down one, disaster overtook him. He never returned to Saintes. He was the first American airman to be awarded the Congressional Medal of Honor in World War I. He had destroyed more planes and balloons than any other American pilot at the time, but he died needlessly. After his shot-up aircraft, with its controls and engine hacked to junk, forced him to land behind the enemy lines, he made a hopeless stand against a platoon of German Infantry. He tried to shoot it out, when he could have surrendered honorably and lived out the last six weeks of the war in a prison compound.

Colonel William Mitchell knew this and resented the useless sacrifice, but he was sincerely touched when he learned of Luke's death. More than anyone else in the A.E.F. he understood the intense drive that had urged the Arizonan to his doom. He had lost a kindred spirit, and when the news came through from Major Hartney he just listened, doodled on his scratch pad, and then said, "Thanks, Harold. I am very sorry to hear it. Good night!"

Colonel Mitchell, alone with his many responsibilities, realized the hopelessness of this kind of warfare. It was poor arithmetic. But more important, on the very night Mitchell had the task of massing almost 200 bomb-carrying aircraft for the Meuse-Argonne offensive; an air attack that was designed to devastate the enemy's rear lines and reserve areas. It was still strictly a tactical intervention in the ground battle, but it gave rise to a prophecy. An Associated Press man wrote:

This navy of the air is to be expanded until no part of Germany is safe from the rain of bombs. It will be a thing apart from the squadrons attached to the various Army corps. Its work will be the bombing of munitions works, factories, cities and other important centers far beyond the German lines.

Billy Mitchell, who became a brigadier general before the Meuse-Argonne offensive was over, had devised massed aerial attacks in that area. Attacks that left the Germans stunned. He had only 1,200 available aircraft, but he handled them so efficiently he kept them flying on important ground-attack missions, enabling General Pershing to move forward rapidly and overrun enemy strong points and heavy-gun emplacements.

He was never able to carry out his strategic aviation plans, but he never gave up the idea that one day he would head an Air Service that would be fully integrated, unified, and operated as a strategic force.

When he finally went home, he took this advanced idea with him.

Chapter 2

AN ERA OF PEACE

GENERAL WILLIAM MITCHELL, one of America's greatest patriots, was born in—of all places—Nice, France. Today a bronze plaque can be seen bolted to the wall of an old house that faces Place Grimaldi. It carries the following inscription:

HERE WAS BORN WILLIAM MITCHELL,
BRIGADIER GENERAL, U. S. ARMY
AIR SERVICE. DECEMBER 29, 1879.

Billy's father, John Lendrum Mitchell, was the son of a Scottish immigrant. John Mitchell and his young wife had gone to the French Riviera for a prolonged vacation. This was a pleasant period of time, when the world was at peace and people who could afford it thought nothing of spending months or years in what today would be regarded as a "foreign" country. International travel was simple and uncomplicated.

There were no passports and few health or immunization requirements.

There was little national rivalry or border bitterness in this period of international peace. The Franco-Prussian War of 1870 had been quickly forgotten, since there were few magazines or illustrated pictorials to rehash the victories or defeats.

On the other side of the Atlantic the first families of America, emerging from the pioneer years with well-established businesses, were amassing fortunes. Many of these people moved freely about Europe, seeking Old World culture and education, or renewing relations with their forebears and their backgrounds.

It was a period of mechanical and scientific marvels both in America and abroad. A form of the telephone had been invented. Primitive phonographs were rasping out tunes and the words of important people. Two Californians, named Muybridge and Isaacs, had made the breakthrough that set the stage for the motion picture. Railroads were spreading their networks in all directions, and this encouraged men and women to travel, see the country, and become acquainted with other people.

Aeronautics was more of a catch phrase than a science, and the aerial accomplishments of that time would be considered prehistoric when compared to modern jet propulsion, transoceanic air lines, missile production and the promise of the conquest of space. But in 1870 Dr. Edmund C. Stedman, a New York scientist, had proposed and designed a rigid airship with many similarities to the global-route Zeppelins of the 1930's.

"Darius Green and his Flying Machine," a popular poem predicting aerial things to come, was written in 1880 by John T. Trowbridge. Thomas Edison was turning his attention to the problems of aviation, and had built a helicopter powered by guncotton. Alexander Graham Bell, who had invented the telephone in 1876, learned that the French were using that instrument from the basket of a captive balloon and employing the combination for military observation. The Tissandier Brothers of Auteuil, France, were actually flying an electrically driven dirigible that used bichromate-of-potash batteries.

Before Billy Mitchell was ten years old, aeronauts all over the world were deserting the inflated gasbags, and risking their necks aboard man-carrying gliders. The airplane was only a dozen years away.

The Mitchell family had seldom been short of money. Billy's grandfather, Alexander Mitchell, had made a fortune with his shrewd business deals, his Wisconsin banks and his investments in the growing American railroads. John Lendrum, Billy's father, did not inherit Alexander's passion for money-making, and in his early years showed signs of becoming a classical scholar. He had been allowed to go to Europe, and had studied in Geneva, Dresden and Munich, but when the Civil War broke out, he quickly returned and willingly volunteered. Later he pioneered in scientific farming. Eventually he built a country home near

Milwaukee where he experimented in crop rotation and soil testing, and bred pedigreed horses and dogs. During these years he also raised a large family.

Billy's father and mother had gone to Nice in search of the Mediterranean sun and to broaden their education. John Lendrum was cosmopolitan in his views, as was his wife, Harriet Danforth Becker, a New York society girl. They stayed in Nice for three years, and their little son spoke much better French than English. Billy's parents had registered him with the American Consular officials to assure his United States' citizenship, but by the time the family had returned to Milwaukee, Billy was completely European. For months he had to live down the taunts of his playmates who called him "Froggie." This so irritated the lad that he refused to speak a word of French for many years.

The new Mitchell home and its surroundings must have been a heaven on earth to a high-spirited boy. "Meadowmere," as it was called, was spread over acres of fine ground. There were ponies to ride, cows to take to pasture, and the barnyard fowls to feed and pet. The farm had a pond on which Billy and his brother and sisters played all kinds of games from high-seas pirates to jungle explorers. They set sail aboard rickety rafts, fished from leaky rowboats, or fought from war canoes that were obviously built to capsize. As a result every youngster in the Mitchell family could swim like a porpoise. It was at Meadowmere that the courage and spirit of young William began to assert itself.

At first, small docile ponies were provided for riding, but gradually larger and more active mounts were brought in. One in particular gave Billy considerable trouble. Day after day this little beast was saddled, and the boy would mount for a canter about the farm. But he usually took a quick toss; the pony would gallop off riderless, and would have to be brought back on a lead halter.

"Mother," admitted Billy one day, "I just can't master that crazy horse."

Most mothers would have comforted the boy, and in their concern and dread of injuries would have agreed that the animal was not safe to ride. Mrs. Mitchell, however, tucked her fears away and said, "He doesn't seem bad tempered to me. You'd better go on riding him until you can show him who is master."

Within a week Billy had the four-legged rogue eating out of his hand.

At Meadowmere there was every opportunity to develop all outdoor skills, and young Mitchell made the most of every lane, thicket, trail, stream and hillock. He tracked with the skill of an Indian. Starting with an air rifle, he developed his marksmanship until he could clip acorns from the top of the tallest oak. He was a good sportsman and never killed for killing's sake. He loved nature and collected a rare assortment of birds' eggs and butterflies. During one trapping season he became so interested in the many species that he decided to save certain specimens. Later he learned taxidermy under the famous Dr. Carl Akeley, at that time in charge of the Milwaukee Museum.

At school Billy became a proficient baseball player, and by the time he was thirteen played polo and was often included in adult line-ups. During the vacation weeks he was the local leader in hunting forays and fishing trips—in any outdoor activity.

But he was not completely one-sided in his pursuits. He took up photography and obtained excellent results. He was an avid reader and usually carried a volume of natural history or some adventure tale in his saddlebags. But more important, he became so engrossed in his activities that he wrote records and lists of his experiences. He kept a diary and poured out pages of his daily life. Not satisfied with recording all this for his own interest, he had to let others know of his life. Lengthy letters went fluttering off in all directions. At first they were childish scribblings with fantastic spelling, but as his interest in so many subjects grew, his skill with words and phrases improved. His many friends were more than willing to encourage him, for they usually received a double donation in the next mail.

This letter writing taught Billy Mitchell the power of words. He was fascinated when he learned that he could interest others in his hobbies and pursuits. Later on he discovered that he could impress these friends with his views, and even sway their opinions on certain subjects. He realized that words had a terrific power when used properly, and as he grew toward manhood he decided to make the most of this talent.

But to write intelligently Billy would need broader

personal experiences in certain fields. Lacking this, he
would have to read everything available, no matter
what the subject. Fortunately, his father and grandfather could provide valuable volumes by many au-
thors, but had the family not been well off, young
Mitchell would have soon discovered the shelves of the
Milwaukee Free Public Library.

Strangely enough, we have no evidence that Billy
was overly interested in aeronautics, although there was
much public display of ballooning in those days. Perhaps he was fascinated by the country-fair daredevils
who went aloft in gaudy hot-air balloons and thrilled
the spectators with their variations of the delayed parachute drop, or brought gasps of anxiety from the
crowds with their capers on trapeze bars slung from
the balloon rigging. He may have flown kites in the
warm spring breezes, but his early history makes no
mention of any particular interest in the new science
on which his colorful career was to focus.

A spirit of independence came honestly to Billy
Mitchell. Early in 1888, when the boy had just turned
eight, his father was chosen to be a member of the Democratic National Committee for Wisconsin. Two years
later he was sent to Congress, and in due course was
elected Senator. His name was placed in nomination
at the Democratic Convention for the Vice-Presidency
of his country.

In the field of social legislation John Lendrum
Mitchell advocated an income tax, favored the eight-
hour day when ten or twelve was the rule, and although

holding a high post in his father's banking empire, was almost radical on the money issue. In 1896 Senator Mitchell boldly supported William Jennings Bryan and his proposal for free and unlimited coinage of silver, which he believed would relieve the economic evils that plagued farmers and factory workers. Remembering the horrors of the Civil War, he spoke continually for disarmament.

Times were uncertain and the financial world went through a difficult phase. In 1893 the Mitchell bank was forced to close and Billy's father voluntarily turned over about $1,350,000—all his cash assets—to enable the institution to get on its feet again and meet all obligations. As a result, the Mitchell family's income was greatly reduced, and now most of it came from the breeding of horses at Meadowmere. Young Billy took a busy hand in this work, turning what had been his prize sport into an important vocation. Fortunately the Mitchells could adjust to this financial letdown, for although they had all been brought up to wealth, there had been a certain Spartan simplicity in their everyday life.

Billy's schooling was typical of the upper middle class of the times. He attended a private school in Milwaukee during his early years, and then Racine College, a preparatory school from which he graduated in 1895. Scholastically he was an average student, but he always made the grade and was able to take part in most sports. He then entered Columbian College, later known as George Washington University in Washington, D.C. He was the youngest student to pass the entrance exams, and during his first year played quarterback and captained the freshman football team.

His summers were routine, but interesting. Some were spent back at Meadowmere, where there were plenty of horses to ride, groom and train. In others the family rented a cottage at Brigantine Beach on the New Jersey coast, where Billy took up and mastered sailing. During one summer vacation the family finances allowed him a student's trip to Europe. There, between visits to famed capitals and Alpine resorts, Billy first felt the undercurrent of international strife.

In Berlin, for instance, a new and very aggressive Kaiser Wilhelm was loudly challenging the British Empire's right to rule the world in benign Victorian manner. Fearing further Prussian aggression, France made a treaty of convenience with the Czar's Russia. The eyes of all the great powers were suddenly focussed on valuable trade possibilities in China, and there was considerable anxiety over the rising power of an island empire known as Japan.

When he returned home, Billy Mitchell discovered that his own Midwest was loudest in the wide plea for world peace. But in the Congress of the United States men were agitating for intervention in Cuba, where rebellion and political terror had raged for years. Strangely enough, Senator Mitchell, a leader in the pursuit of world peace and disarmament, sympathized with the Cuban rebels who were valiantly trying to throw off the European yoke of Spain. On June 9, 1897, while addressing the graduating class of Columbian College, the elder Mitchell pointed out Switzerland as a model for all Europe.

"Why can't these European countries federate themselves together under a similar government?" he demanded. "That little nation spent more on education than on military service, while the rest of Europe pays out fourteen times more for its armed forces than it does for education. These nations do not differ more radically than the cantons of Switzerland. Why can't they reorganize and erase this great folly of war?"

Military glory had little place in the thinking of Senator Mitchell, and it was generally agreed that Europe was a hotbed of international conflict. But only ten months elapsed before the United States found itself swept into a war with Spain. Soon Admiral Dewey was to win his great victory on the other side of the Pacific, a triumph that left America forging a link between the farthest West and the farthest East, fated to act as a balance of power among the great nations of the world. In other words, American isolation, so revered in the Middle West, was obliterated by Admiral Dewey's conquest in Manila Bay. The American commonwealth was now a far-flung empire.

Billy Mitchell shook off his adolescence to face a world the like of which he had never known or imagined. A man named Professor Samuel P. Langley, a friend of General Adolphus W. Greely, a famous explorer of that day, had demonstrated a heavier-than-air model plane that had flown for more than half a mile. This invention was a tandem monoplane, sixteen feet long, with a wingspan of thirteen feet. A tiny 1½ hp steam engine turned twin propellers, and the model was launched from a catapult mounted on top of a Potomac River houseboat. With this assisted take-off the monoplane flew a distance of 3,200 feet in a series of graceful, sweeping curves. When the water supply for the engine was exhausted, the model made a beautiful three-point landing on the river.

This flight was most satisfactory. Afterward Langley believed that a man-carrying version could be built and flown. Theodore Roosevelt, then Assistant Secretary of the Navy, willingly headed a group that induced the government to allot a Congressional fund of $50,000 to continue the experiments.

Warm interest was aroused, but not without considerable high-level prodding. Dr. Alexander Graham Bell was most enthused with Professor Langley's invention, and with Theodore Roosevelt representing the Navy and General Greely the Army, President McKinley found himself advocating the development of heavier-than-air machines for military combat.

This early enthusiasm for the airplane soon lagged. The Navy was too involved with activity in the Pacific, and Teddy Roosevelt left Washington to head the Rough Riders, who were to make history in Cuba. Only General Greely stayed on to push the project and actually see that Professor Langley was given full co-operation—a point that would have been missed had not a young man named William Mitchell said, in writing Greely's biography some years later:

"Even though this money had been made available, it was with the greatest difficulty that Greely persuaded Langley to continue the work."

The famous scientist evidently did not wish to disparage, through any possible failure, his international reputation. However, General Greely insisted, cajoled, and begged Langley to go on, and eventually the famous man-carrying "aerodrome," as it was called, was built.

This machine was capable of controlled flight, but that was not proven immediately. Two unknown bicycle repairmen from Dayton, Ohio, were to gain the honor of being the first to invent and fly a heavier-than-air machine—the Wright biplane. Even the Wrights agreed that "the knowledge that the head of the most prominent scientific institution in America [Langley] believed in the possibility of human flight, was one of the influences that led us to undertake the preliminary investigations that preceded our active work. He recommended to us the books that enabled us to form sound ideas at the outset. It was a helping hand at a critical time, and we shall always be grateful."

Billy Mitchell was convinced that General Greely's belief in Professor Langley led to America's leadership in the air. The general's faith in the conquests of science deeply impressed this young man, and over the years he was to fully appreciate Greely's bold sponsorship in the face of resistance from other military experts who refused to believe in the heavier-than-air machine. Who knows? It may have been General Greely who thus unwittingly produced America's "stormy petrel," Billy Mitchell.

Chapter 3

THE DRUMS OF WAR

B<small>ILLY</small> M<small>ITCHELL</small>'s pleasant world of peace and domestic tranquility came to an end in the spring of 1898. War was in the air. On April 24 of that year the spectator's gallery in the United States Senate was crowded with anxious visitors, and as they hurried from one aisle to another their footsteps took on the cadence of marching troops.

Spain had offered Cuba the right of self-government, but the insurgents had determined to fight for full freedom. The U. S. Navy battleship *Maine* had been mysteriously blown up in Havana harbor. President McKinley, who had been appealing for an armistice, suddenly moved for a declaration of war against Spain.

Billy Mitchell, now eighteen, huddled in the gallery as he listened to the words of important men—those of his father among them—and awaited the adoption of a resolution that would call the nation to arms. A few days before, an act had been passed that authorized the enlistment of volunteer troops.

Realizing that his father hated war and all it signified, Billy awaited the vote. He saw war as only a glorious action, just as it had been depicted in his story books. War meant cavalry charges, spiking enemy guns, the brave stands against ambush and the eventual rewards of military decorations, dress uniforms and the satisfaction of having done one's bit.

The minute the United States declared war on Spain, Billy tore out of the Senate gallery and hurried to his home, a stone's throw away. The Senate Office building now stands on that plot.

Later when his father came home with several colleagues, Billy strode down the wide stairway, solemn and determined.

"Hello, Son," Senator Mitchell said with a weary tone in his voice. "Where are you going?"

Without waiting for the other Senators to withdraw, Billy said defiantly, "Father, now that we are at war, I am going to enlist."

"Enlist? But you haven't finished college."

"You did the same. You gave up your education to get into the Civil War. You voted for war today. I saw you, although I knew you were for disarmament."

"I had very little choice, Son."

"You did your duty as you saw it. Now I want to do mine."

Someone broke in with: "Do you mean to say you

would enlist as a private? If you finish college, you could get a commission."

"I'm not interested in a commission," Billy snapped. "I'm quite willing to begin as a private. A good many people do. I'm going to join your old regiment, Father, the First Wisconsin Infantry."

At this point Mrs. Mitchell moved into the group from another room. She had six other children, but Billy was the oldest and her beloved first-born. Still, she knew that one day he would make his fledgling flight from her nest. She started to voice her objections, but one look from that erect young man standing at the bottom of the staircase melted all her words. She was proud, and moved over to his side.

Senator Joseph Wheeler, a one-time Confederate general, remonstrated with Senator Mitchell, "But, John, you're not going to let this *little* boy go to war?"

It was this statement that clinched Billy's future.

Senator Mitchell bristled and said, "Why not? He's eighteen. He's sound mentally and physically. Of course, I shall let him go."

Someone spoke up and said that Billy need not enlist. Since he was a college student, he could apply for and gain a commission in one of the militia regiments. Senator Mitchell shook his head at this suggestion, and turned to his wife.

"He has my permission, Harriet, but I won't let him go unless he has yours. What do you say?"

Mrs. Mitchell knew her favorite son too well. She knew that he would go no matter what her decision;

he would not even wait for an officer's commission. There was nothing else to do, so she just smiled, led Billy back upstairs, and helped him pack his bag.

The young man's introduction to military life must have been appalling. Selective-service recruits today enjoy luxury conditions compared to what greeted Billy at an improvised militia camp outside Milwaukee that spring. The undergraduate, who had so long enjoyed the best of everything, wore a makeshift uniform, slopped around in mud, slept on the ground or in shelters that had no screens to keep out flies and mosquitoes.

Never one to hold his peace, Billy started a new letter-writing campaign. "You never saw such sanitation," he wrote in one outburst. "Our latrines, garbage cans and trash heaps are stacked up beside the company kitchens. Can you imagine that? There are flies that have been here for months and know more military drill and procedure than we do. When mess call rings out, they swarm off the garbage heaps, do 'squads left,' and head straight for the mess shack and form up on our food. Some of the boys are already suffering from typhoid fever, malaria and about every filth disease known. Of the original nine men in my tent, only three of us have stayed out of hospital."

Young Mitchell was drilled in the manual of arms with an old Springfield .45-caliber rifle that used black powder. A weapon improved very little over the muskets used in the Civil War. At the same time, the

Spaniards in Cuba were equipped with ultramodern Mausers.

After some three weeks of recruit training, the First Wisconsin Infantry was shipped down to Tampa, a jumping-off spot for the Cuban War. In that short time, despite the ill-fitting uniform and the strain of rigorous living, Billy had taken on a new military bearing and walked as proudly as a peacock.

His spirit did not escape the attention of General Greely who personally recommended young Mitchell for a commission. As a result Private Mitchell was called out of his tent one day and ordered to proceed to Washington.

"What for?" Private Mitchell demanded. "I just came from there."

"You've been recommended for a commission," his superior explained loftily.

"But I didn't ask for a commission, sir."

"I'm afraid you have no choice. General Greely signed the order."

With crushed hopes, Billy returned to Washington, and was assigned immediately as a second lieutenant to the 2nd Volunteer Signal Company. Before he had time to become used to his new uniform, he was sent out to suppress a serious riot that had been staged by a number of disgruntled soldiers who were being shipped south. There were no Military Police, as we know them today.

The rioters, ignoring all orders, had deserted a troop train, swarmed into the city, and taken over the bar

and kitchen of the American House. There, under the
influence of drink, they wrecked the furniture, ejected
every hotel worker, and terrorized the patrons. As fast
as civil policemen moved in to arrest them, they were
beaten up and tossed out of the building.

Second Lieutenant Mitchell handled this situation
superbly, making the most of his new rank. First he
lined up fourteen soldiers, armed with .45-caliber car-
bines, outside the hotel. Then with a college friend,
Robert Sterrett, and a massive N.C.O., Billy strode
boldly into the main bar. No one took any notice of
him. The place was a shambles. Men were making
drinks and tossing empty bottles at the bar mirror,
much in the manner of the traditional Western melo-
drama.

Suddenly Second Lieutenant Mitchell bellowed:
"Attention!"

When the bleary-eyed rioters saw this tight-lipped
young lieutenant glaring at them, they all stood up.
One or two immediately fell down, but they were
yanked to their feet by Sterrett or the burly N.C.O.

"Outside, all of you," Mitchell roared. "Line up out
there immediately!"

"They were in bad shape," Billy wrote later to his
mother, "so I decided to march them into condition. It
was a very hot day and it was about three miles to the
Washington barracks, but I made sure they marched
every yard. Oh, I picked up a couple of firemen who
had hydrant wrenches, so they could cool off, or quench

their thirsts. When we arrived at the barracks there wasn't a drunken man in the bunch."

Once the mob was safe and under guard, Billy wrote a formal account which reached the desk of General Greely, head of the Signal Corps. A few days later Billy was asked to report to the general.

"You did a fine job, son," General Greely said and smiled. "That was a very good report—once I had interpreted it. You write a fine hand, but I must say your spelling and punctuation are hair-raising at times."

"I'm sorry, sir. I'll see what I can do about that."

"Good! In the meantime you'd better go pack your gear. You will report immediately to Camp Cuba Libre in Jacksonville, Florida."

But active service in Cuba was not in the book for Billy Mitchell. Most of that summer was spent in routine training under the burning sun, and although he tried every known trick to get across the Straits of Florida, delay followed delay. In his exasperation Billy wrote a series of scathing letters in which he criticized everyone from the President down. He was positive that soldiers who did manage to get over had some mysterious influence with higher officials.

And as always, Billy noted that those who wanted to go were denied the right, while others who were selected immediately lost their patriotism and gold-bricked to seek less hazardous assignments.

The storm hawk was getting his pinfeathers.

The war in Cuba soon petered out, and before Mitchell's outfit could see any foreign service, Spain was suing for peace. By then it looked as though he would soon be out of uniform and on his way back to college. But while awaiting the decisions of his superiors, Billy continued to work hard, learning the many jobs required by the Signal Corps. At mid-August he was second in command of the Cuba Libre camp, and two months later had charge of a company that laid a Pablo Beach telegraph line in record time. He had mastered signal code, and had carried out all forms of signal operations, except balloon observation. He had also taught himself the use of the typewriter by writing his letters home in this manner. In what spare time he could find he continued his study of physics and trigonometry and even took up Spanish.

When all hope of getting to Cuba had vanished and Billy had accepted his fate, his company suddenly received orders to sail with other units to serve in the Army of Occupation, an organization set up to restore law and order on the island. He landed at Camp Columbia, Havana, on December 24, and considered that the finest Christmas present he had ever received.

Before the year was out Cuba had been liberated and taken under the protecting arm of the United States. Puerto Rico and Guam were ceded to America as indemnity, and the Philippines were surrendered for a payment of $20,000,000. As we know now, Guam became a U. S. naval base, and Manila the capital of our new Colonial domain.

In reply to those who resented this Pacific annexation, President McKinley said, "We had little choice. The United States would have become the laughing-stock of the world if we had not taken the Philippines." He concluded that message with: "And so it has come to pass that in a few short months we have become a world power."

When the Spanish flag was run down from the staff of the Governor-General's Palace in Havana and the Stars and Stripes hauled up in its place, Billy Mitchell believed that ceremony to be the most important event in the history of his country since the surrender at Yorktown.

But while reflecting, Billy kept busy, and in learning Spanish could slowly pick out the main stories in the Havana newspapers. He was able to talk to people on the street, and soon formed strong opinions as to the destiny of Cuba. Although he grew to like the general public and appreciate its industry, he observed later that not all Cubans admired their American liberators.

"I noticed that when we first arrived they seemed very glad to see us," he wrote to his parents, "but after a few weeks I sensed a definite change."

His father, in Washington, was pleased with the Spanish evacuation of the West Indies, and believed that the Cuban question was no longer a thorn in America's side. Lieutenant Mitchell disagreed, feeling that Cuba would be a problem in the future.

How keenly Billy Mitchell was thinking, and how his views fit the present situation, more than sixty years

later, make interesting reading. But perhaps this viewpoint was influenced by his continued study of the
great military campaigns of history.

In the early spring of 1899 insurrection broke out in
the Philippines under the leadership of Emilio Aguinaldo, a rebel who believed that the Philippines should
be given full freedom, now that the Spanish yoke had
been cast off. American troops were again thrown into
action, and continually cut down in cruel jungle fighting, ambush and savage retaliation.

Billy Mitchell lost all interest in Cuba, the possibility of a military discharge, or even a promised vacation in France. Instead, he applied for a transfer, and
begged his father to use his influence with General
Greely. However, it was Mrs. Mitchell who interceded
for her son.

General Greely was sympathetic, but pointed out
that Lieutenant Mitchell was needed in Cuba. He had
already strung up 138 miles of telegraph lines, and because of his energy, ability and intelligence had been
invited to join the staff of General Fitzhugh Lee, in
Havana, as his assistant chief signal officer. Billy argued
that he would relinquish his commission if necessary,
and "face the enemy" as a private. He tried every ruse
and angle until at last his father made a special plea
in his behalf.

Lieutenant Mitchell got his orders to leave for the
Philippines early in July. This route took him through
Puerto Rico, Santo Domingo, Haiti and Washington.

There he met his father who was preparing to join the family in France where they were again on vacation.

On a stopover at Milwaukee, on the way to San Francisco, Billy was greeted by many of his young friends, including the MacArthur boys. General Arthur MacArthur, a friend of the Mitchell family, was then in command of a division in the Philippines, and one of his sons, Douglas, some four weeks younger than Billy, had just been accepted for West Point. At one of their parties, someone said:

"You know, Billy, you will be among the reinforcements, and you will have to be prepared to go into action immediately."

Billy laughed. "It can't come too soon for me. That's what I joined up for."

The prediction turned out to be true. Within thirty-six hours after arriving at Manila, young Mitchell and the other American troops were on their way to the battle front. Their assignment: to surround and close in on General Emilio Aguinaldo's army. Three columns, under Generals MacArthur, Lawton and Wheaton, were engaged in this campaign. Billy was assigned to MacArthur's division.

The main problem in putting down the insurrection was to capture the wily leader, Aguinaldo, and the American forces got off to a bad start when General Lawton's column lost contact with the other two divisions. A new telegraph system had to be evolved and erected to remedy this situation, and of course this task fell to Lieutenant Mitchell.

"You have a real problem," General MacArthur explained, "but it has to be done. Lawton may be seventy-five miles away."

"We have enough transmitting instruments, sir," Lieutenant Mitchell said cheerfully. "I'll have to manufacture some batteries and get wire and insulators from heaven knows where, but I think we can manage."

"Get going, Lieutenant!"

Young Mitchell commandeered every foot of barbed wire available, and then discovered that some of the cannon that had been captured from the insurgents were wire-wound—a process employed to strengthen the barrels. He set a couple of privates to unwinding them and putting the wire on reels, while he himself turned to the problem of batteries.

There were some old Spanish battery cells available, but he had no sal ammoniac (ammonium chloride) to provide the chemical reaction necessary in dry cells.

"What was I to do?" Billy said later. "I went to the field kitchen and 'borrowed' all their table salt. It produced a current but it was so weak we could detect it only by putting the terminal wires to our tongues. However, it turned out to be sufficient to work the dot-and-dash receiver."

Transportation was his next problem, so he bargained for the use of twenty water buffalo. Packsaddles were made out of hemp and dried banana leaves. With this "Rube Goldberg" equipment Billy Mitchell set off to find General Lawton and get him and his division back into the War.

No one expected to see Mitchell and his small party again, but the Wisconsin boy made a gay adventure of the hazardous undertaking.

The route through the jungle was heartbreaking, and the natives encountered not too friendly. Lieutenant Mitchell sensed that as soon as they realized what his wire and bottle tops were for they would quickly cut them down and braid the tangle into tribal ornaments. With his Spanish and some wild pantomime Billy soon made it plain that if any of this telegraph wire was removed or damaged, he would burn down every hut and cattle shed within a mile of the break.

The telegraph line stayed up.

In the meantime his Signal Corps crew worked like demons, stringing up the wire and making tests. When the supply of bottle tops was exhausted, they used dried bamboo tubes for insulators. Hacking through the jungle and across hard ground, they strung this wire over a distance of nearly seventy-five miles.

But they found General Lawton.

The general could hardly believe his eyes until Billy tapped out a message to General MacArthur and received a reply.

"I still don't understand how you got here," General Lawton repeated. "And your makeshift telegraph is a miracle!"

"The miracle's all yours, General," Billy said, and

crawled away to find a bed. The rest of his men were already asleep.

With General Lawton and his column back on the team, the net was spread again for Aguinaldo, and most of his main force was cut up into scattered groups. The leader, however, escaped by slipping through the American lines disguised as a Chinaman. Actually, "Aggie," as he was known, had managed to work his way well up into northern Luzon where he held out for more than a year.

By the time he was twenty Billy Mitchell was Acting Chief Signal Officer of General MacArthur's division. His work took him into danger spots day after day, but he always carried out his assignment. He studied Tagalog, the chief tribal language of the Philippines, and with this at his command became friendly with many native leaders.

Whenever he gained their confidence he would ask, "Where is the *insurrecto* camp?" One of these inquiries provided a nubbin of a clue, so Mitchell ordered two Filipino natives to accompany him on a series of night reconnaissances. He found Aguinaldo's hide-out, then commanded by Captain Mendoza, Aguinaldo's chief aide. The next night Billy moved in with fifteen volunteers and captured Mendoza before the insurgents could get to their arms. Even more important, Lieutenant Mitchell came away with military documents that outlined some details of Aguinaldo's underground organization and gave a hint as to where he might be found.

For this enterprise Billy Mitchell was promoted to first lieutenant.

Meanwhile, time after time, "Aggie" slipped out of the traps that were set for him. He treated the natives harshly if he thought they were co-operating with the Americans; and in the campaign to run him to earth, many skirmishes took place, some of which were unusually expensive.

Colonel Frederick Funston, a little-known soldier of fortune, held a commission in the Volunteers. He was a self-taught soldier. He had been in the Philippines for some time and was about to be sent home for mustering out. A free-and-easy man, he was a fascinating character on active service and young Mitchell became one of his ardent admirers.

Colonel Funston had fought in Cuba long before America had taken up the cause. He had traveled a great deal and prospected in Alaska prior to the Gold Rush. His stories were endless, and Billy sought out this colorful colonel whenever possible.

Strange to relate, within a short time, aided in no small way by Lieutenant Mitchell, Colonel Funston was able to execute the most important single military exploit of the year.

Aguinaldo was still on the loose, foiling every effort to capture him. The Philippine campaign simmered down to guerrilla fighting, and in Washington was being considered an unfinished war. To many it seemed that only Colonel Funston, Lieutenant Mitchell of the Signal Corps and Lieutenant J. D. Taylor, who was in charge of the few remaining troops on the chase, had any particular interest in the capture of "Aggie."

In the fall of 1900, Lieutenant Mitchell was stationed at Pantabangan, and after interrogating the mayor of the town, picked up some idea of where Aguinaldo might be hiding. So he started on another of his small-party scoutings, hauling telegraph wire with him wherever he went. In a short time he had a veritable network of communications linked up, and was able eventually to pinpoint "Aggie's" actual position.

Again he asked permission to go in and get him, just as he had done in capturing Mendoza. But General MacArthur refused. He felt that Billy was too young for such an important mission, and pointed out that he was due to return to the United States for a furlough and possibly a new assignment.

The capture of Aguinaldo was entrusted to Colonel Funston. Lieutenant Mitchell received his orders to return to the United States by way of the Orient and Europe.

Shortly after Mitchell's departure, Colonel Funston moved in and trapped the wily Aguinaldo. For this exploit he was made a brigadier general, and in 1914 became a major general in charge of American troops on the Mexican border.

Chapter 4

THE FROZEN NORTH

FOLLOWING his adventures in the Philippines, Billy Mitchell had a restful, easygoing return trip through Asia and Europe. On the way he promoted a military observer's view of the Boxer Rebellion, in which a combined force of American, British, French, German, Russian and Japanese troops put down a Chinese uprising aimed to drive all white traders out of China. Billy believed that this would be his last experience in a shooting war and when he reached America he felt that his service days were over. To hear Bill tell it, he was already a doddering old veteran at twenty-one, ready to retire to his fireside corner and there retell the tales of his campaigns.

He wrote his mother, who was in Germany with the rest of the family, that he planned to return to civilian life and would join them as soon as possible. However, his brother and sisters were dismayed at this news.

Their swashbuckling hero's letters had been much more fun than their geography and history books. They were so dramatic and lively, and written in such master-scene style, that it was easy to cut them up into individual parts and play out his adventures for visiting friends and school companions.

But first there were routine matters for Billy to complete, reports to make and official farewells to be said. He hurried to Washington with his letter of resignation in his pocket, to pay his respects to his superior, General Greely.

Lieutenant Mitchell was greeted warmly, for he was one of the general's favorites. "You look a trifle peaked, Son," the general commented as they shook hands.

"I've had a touch of malaria, sir, but it's nothing serious."

"I'm glad to know that. You did a fine job out there. I'd like to take a few minutes to talk over a few personal matters. I liked your reports."

Billy grinned. "How was the spelling, sir?"

"You've improved wonderfully. How did . . . ?"

"I keep a pocket dictionary nearby, sir," Lieutenant Mitchell confessed, with another broad grin.

As Billy fumbled for his letter of resignation, the general interrupted with: "If you feel rested, I think I have something that might interest you, Lieutenant."

"I had thought of joining the family—in Germany."

"I have a bag of trouble up in Alaska. How would you like to go up North? There's no malaria there."

Young Mitchell jerked to an erect position. He heard

little of what the general was saying; his mind had
reverted to his nights with Colonel Funston in the
Philippines when the old adventurer had spun tales
that seeped through the shadows of the big room.
Alaska—the explorer's dream. New, fantastic territory
that had been purchased from Russia in 1867, and
then left to lie dormant, since no one knew what to do
with it. Thirty years later a placer gold mine had
opened up the Klondike, and Alaska, once known as
"Seward's Icebox," suddenly became another hot chest-
nut for the United States Government to handle.

"We have a few troops up there," Greely was saying
as Bill came out of his reverie, "but we have no communications. Every day new stakes are being made. It's
not only gold, but fish, furs, lumber and many other
natural resources. The place is full of tough, reckless
men, and we have little means of maintaining law and
order. What happens in Nome is not known in Juneau
until weeks later."

"It's very close to Siberia, isn't it?" Billy said to keep
the conversation going.

"You're right. A good observation, Bill. Alaska can
become the chief strategic-command point of the Pacific. Take a look at that map there."

Billy shoved his letter deeper into his pocket. "You
want someone to go up there?"

"We've been trying to put a telegraph line across
that country to link up the principal cities. So far, no
luck. We have army posts at important points, but
there's no way of getting messages to or from them. Can

you believe this? When things get out of hand, we have to call in Canada's Northwest Mounted Police to come across the border and help handle the situation!"

"Humiliating," Bill commented as he ran his finger along the Alaskan coast line and out across the islands of the Aleutian chain.

"We can't even telegraph to Washington from Alaska," Greely said with some bitterness in his voice.

Mitchell turned from the map. "It's very cold up there, I'm told."

"Cold? The temperature can drop to seventy degrees below zero. There are no roads to speak of; just trails. Wheeled transportation is out of the question most of the time. The short summers are hot and turn the country into a bog. Then winter sets in and everyone up there hibernates—like the bears. It seems impossible to get anything done."

Billy set his jaw. "It can't be that tough. Anything I can do, sir?"

General Greely looked relieved. "I want someone to make a preliminary survey. I want to know whether a telegraph line can be put up. If you say it can, you had better be right, because I shall send you back at once and make you put it up. I don't want you to toady to me, and then leave the job to someone else. You want to go to Alaska, Lieutenant?"

Mitchell pulled the letter from his pocket and tore it into small squares as the general looked puzzled. "That was my letter of resignation, sir," Bill explained, and tossed the shreds into the waste basket. "When do I start?"

"What are we waiting for?" the general responded.

On July 31, 1901, Bill wrote his mother: "I'm still a soldier. I am to go to Alaska on a special detail. It could be a whizzer. Can you imagine me, not yet twenty-two, being second in command in Alaska—a country more than half the size of the United States? It's sort of dizzying."

His brother John and his sisters immediately made plans for a new series of home-grown dramas—all set in the Frozen North.

Lieutenant William Mitchell selected a detachment of Signal Corps men from Fort Myer, Virginia, collected all the necessary equipment and made his way to Seattle, Washington. On the way he learned that one of his chief problems would be the recruiting of civilian labor. In Alaska a worker could get from one to three dollars an hour. He couldn't get that much a day in the States. Bill figured that digging a post hole in that frozen ground would take most of a day, and to dig a single hole might cost as much as eight dollars.

"Boy, at that rate, I may have to recruit some Chinese coolies," he reflected.

But Bill pushed that problem from his mind, and moved on to Skagway, a short distance north of Juneau. From there he planned to work his way over the White Pass to the headwaters of the Yukon in Canada, move down the Yukon through Dawson, by-pass the White

Horse Rapids, and head west until he reached St. Michael on the Norton Sound Coast where a United States military post had been established. This trip would be a trek of more than 2,500 miles through wild country.

Young Mitchell buttonholed everyone who had ever been in the Gold Rush, hoping to learn something of the people and the country. The most important piece of information he collected was that he could expect every man in his detachment to desert once they reached the placer country.

"You think they're gonner dig postholes up there for the Army's fifteen-dollars-a-month, when they could make a million working their own claims?" one experienced sourdough queried.

Mitchell talked over this serious problem with his Sergeant Pollner. They decided that there was only one way to head off any mass desertion. Bill laid it on the line and demanded complete loyalty, while Pollner tightened his discipline. As a result, not one soldier went A.W.O.L. Every man who went aboard the wooden steamer *Cottage Queen* and headed for the Yukon, served out his time; each one soon realized that he was in for a fabulous experience.

The extremes in the Alaskan climate are almost unbelievable. The Japanese Current bathes the Aleutian Islands and all of the southern part of Alaska's 26,000 miles of coast line. It warms the air, bringing moisture and tremendous downfalls of rain and snow. More than eighty feet of snow were measured in Thompson Pass that winter. In the southern area the climate is more bearable, vegetation is fairly luxuriant, and many grains, grasses and vegetables can easily be grown.

In the Yukon watershed and along the 2,200 miles of navigable river, the weather conditions are wild and rugged. The Alaska Range, the highest on the continent, and the Coast Range, almost as lofty, shut off the mellow warmth of the Pacific. The temperature falls as low as anywhere in the world, but the air is too cold to hold moisture and the snowfall is not too heavy. When Southern Alaska is shrouded in fog and lashed by rains and snowstorms, the interior, with its almost six months of frozen night, is calm and clear. If any high winds could scream across this area, nothing could survive.

It was into this inhospitable world Bill was to tramp, taking his first surveys to establish a network of communications that would enable a handful of U. S. Army men to bring law and order to this vast Northern territory.

Once his party had arrived at Skagway, Bill took a few days to look around and get his bearings. He found the town alive with roughneck miners, some of whom had made a strike. But all too many were disheartened, penniless, and ready for anything that would bring in a quick dollar. The saloons were filled with crooks, cardsharps, ex-convicts and anyone who couldn't make a decent living in legal employment. Anything could inflame this mob to a violence that would threaten the whole settlement.

A primitive railroad, only recently completed, crawled out of Skagway and ran to White Horse, about 120 miles north. This line was competing with wheeled freighters hauled by horses and mules. Here the spirit of the area was as unlawful as might be expected. On one occasion Bill had to talk fast and tough to a freight manager who offered him 10 per cent of whatever the government paid for haulage.

"You jest give us the job, soldier, and we'll see you get your cut," the man said and winked.

"Nothing doing. You're picking on the wrong soldier," Bill snapped. "Not only that, I'll see that you haul nothing for us as long as the railroad turns a wheel. We don't work that way, mister."

The turbulent White Horse Rapids break the navigation for steamboats, and Bill had to portage his men and gear around the water barrier to a little wood-burning steamer that chugged north to Dawson City in Canada. There members of the Northwest Mounted Police greeted the party and saw that every help was given the American soldiers. It was summer and the weather was better than reasonable, but the Canadians warned that by midwinter the temperatures would drop to between 60 and 70 degrees below zero.

"In that case," young Mitchell reflected, "we'll have to move along the next sixteen hundred miles of river pretty fast, before it freezes up."

Captain Scarth of the Mounties suggested that Bill

buy or build a flatboat on which to haul his equipment and supplies. This was a sound idea, for at that point the river was deep and swift-flowing, moving at about eight miles an hour. The banks were alive with big game, and the water abounded in several kinds of salmon, trout and ling. The lakes in the basin would provide pike, pickerel and other species of trout. All told, and considering the game ducks and geese, it was a hunter's paradise; but more important, it assured Bill that they would never starve.

When all this planning was completed, Bill next decided how he would survey the area for the proposed telegraph line. He mapped out a line from Eagle City, well inside the Alaskan border, to run to the south and end at Valdez on Prince William Sound. Another leg would stretch westward from Eagle City, follow the Yukon and have its terminus at St. Michael on the west coast. This was simply a survey. No wire was to be strung.

Accompanied by a couple of guides and some pack horses, Bill started out, but his party soon ran into long stretches of moss that were so soft the horses sank in well above their knees if they carried any load at all. Bill soon realized that to attempt such transport in the summer was almost impossible, since under such conditions, each pack horse would be able to carry less than 200 pounds.

It was at this point that Mitchell figured out the secret of working in the Arctic.

"This is ridiculous," he mused. "We cannot spend

this sort of time and money. But if we did the heavy-load moving in the winter, we could use sleds that could haul at least a ton. We could move twenty-five to thirty miles a day."

He made the suggestion to one of the guides, who laughed. "That's fine, but who can you get to work outdoors in the winter? The folks up here 'hole in.' No one can work outside in those temperatures."

"Has it ever been tried?" Bill demanded.

"Well . . . no. I don't think *I'd* want to risk it. You take one look at the thermometer next winter. You'd be crazy to go outdoors."

"But suppose we provided suitable clothing, proper shelter and good food—a real man ought to be able to keep alive," Bill challenged. "I should think he'd work fine, just so long as he kept moving."

The guide scratched his head. "Maybe you got the money, Lieutenant. Maybe you could get a few people who need money, but I doubt it."

"Look," Bill began again with mounting enthusiasm, "why wouldn't it be possible to work reasonable hours through the winter? I just want to get the material out. The poles, wire and insulators could be stored along the route. The food supplies and forage for the horses could be cached at suitable intervals. It would be easy when the ground is firm, and we have snow for sleds."

The guide nodded with weakening opposition.

"Then in the summer, when the ground has softened, we could dig the holes, erect the poles, and get the line strung under pleasant conditions. Get it?"

"I get it, Lieutenant. But can you do it?"

"That is how it is going to be done," Bill snapped. "Let's go!"

Over the rest of that summer Lieutenant Mitchell and his party continued to survey, and by the end of August he noted the first frost on the ridges. The bears showed signs of hibernating, and the salmon had stopped running in the river. On his arrival back at Eagle City, he had his plan complete. Now he decided that the westward line would run along the Tenana River, skirt the Yukon, run to the Bering Sea, and have its final terminus at Nome.

When the plan was announced, the sourdoughs, miners and Klondike drifters had the best laugh of the season. "Why the poor fool! What does he think he's doing? He's had a few weeks of summer in Alaska and now he knows everything. Just wait and see what Alaska does to him."

Lieutenant Billy laughed with them—a trick that always bewilders critics—but he stuck to his plan. Once he had the general idea of how the line was to be built, he put his gear aboard an old river steamer known as *Sarah* and continued down the Yukon to trace out a general route for the western loop.

It was getting late in the year, and he decided to get a taste of what an Alaskan winter could be like. As they churned west day after day the country changed, the trees were smaller, the mountains grim and stark and the Indians were replaced by Eskimos. Parkas were now made of fur, not cloth, and there was as much interest in the trapping trade, as in the wild-and-wooly gold digging.

No time was wasted anywhere. Mitchell studied the way boats and rafts were built. The customs of the natives and their primitive workmanship fascinated him. He collected carved ivory and Eskimo drawings, and bought a fine collection of native furs to take home to his family. Nothing escaped his eye or pen, and his letters furnished a hundred new scenes of the northland wastes, the history of a dozen blizzard-beaten towns and drawings of Eskimo villages. He traced out their habits, marriage ceremonies, details of their shelters, boats and hunting weapons.

Eventually the *Sarah* threaded her way through the Yukon delta that fingers into the Bering Sea, and at last reached the end of the trip at St. Michael, a settlement commanding the mouth of the river. It had once been a Russian post, but in 1901 was taken over as the headquarters of the United States Army in the North.

Bill rested here for a short time to complete his notes, then hurried down to Seattle where he made a full report to General Greely. This paper was typical of Mitchell's enthusiasm, but worded in a manner that might have enraged others who had gone before him.

"There's no reason why this telegraph line can't be put up," Mitchell said. "Those who have tried before and failed stayed indoors too much in the winter. You have to work the year around. I believe the whole two thousand two hundred miles could be strung in about two years."

General Greely was amused at the brashness of his favorite lieutenant, changed the appraisal to four years, and issued the full report to the American press. It was published all over the country, and the young Signal Corps dynamo was thus introduced to the American public. They were to hear much from him over the next thirty-five years.

The general soon sent his response on to Seattle. "Thanks for your report and confidence," he wired. "Get back here as soon as possible."

Eventually, this amazing winter project was placed under direct charge of General Randall, but Lieutenant Mitchell was entrusted with the building of a major portion of the system. His section would connect up with a Canadian line terminating at Dawson City.

During this time there was a world-wide revival in aeronautics. A Brazilian coffee millionaire, Santos-Dumont, had flown a small dirigible (powered with a 3½ hp gasoline engine) over Paris, and circled the Eiffel Tower to win a prize of 125,000 francs. At the same time Count Ferdinand von Zeppelin was flying a rigid airship, the first of the long series of Zeppelins, over Lake Constance on the German-Swiss border. This was the beginning of the lighter-than-air fleet that was destined to sail all skies in peace and war. In 1901 two German scientists, Dr. R. Suring and a Professor Berson, flew a spherical balloon to a height of 34,424 feet—or a distance of about seven miles. These early aeronauts carried oxygen tanks to sustain them at this amazing height.

That same year Comte Henri de la Valux, a Parisian financier, made the first aerial crossing of the Mediterranean in a balloon, carrying three companions with him. Starting from Toulon at 6:30 A.M. one day, the party landed in Algeria shortly after 4 P.M.

Having read of this in the Portland *Oregonian,* Billy raced through all the bookstores in Seattle and gathered every volume on aeronautics then available. He took all of these with him to Alaska. At the time he explained airily: "I just like to have something to read. Who knows, they might be of help when I take my captaincy examinations?"

A very interesting comment, considering that within two years the Wright Brothers would make the first heavier-than-air flight at Kitty Hawk.

Chapter 5

DEEP FREEZE

Just as soon as he was given the "Go Ahead" signal, Lieutenant Mitchell put in orders for two years' supplies, and spent days hand-picking his assistants from the best troops stationed at Portland, Oregon and the Vancouver Barracks, Washington. Wisely, he selected several tough, self-reliant men who were twice his age—knowing that he needed a certain amount of sage experience to balance the impetuosity of youth. As it turned out, he selected well. Not one of his company failed him in the hazardous months ahead.

Within three weeks he was ready to head north with his second party, and when they arrived at Juneau the long night had fallen. The great canneries had closed down. A grim silence had settled over the Northland. It was November, and in addition to the cold and gloom of the country, Bill had to listen to the woes of Major Field, an old Spanish War friend who had been attempting to lay an undersea cable from Juneau to Skagway. Major Field had experienced all the troubles that come from lack of good labor and an overabundance of bad weather.

In addition, Major Field's civilian contractor, in order to figure the distance between any two points, had drawn a line on the waterway chart and measured the mileage from the scale. He had failed to realize that distances "as the ship sails" are a great deal shorter than the mileage over the underwater mountain peaks and valleys. Major Field was short by more than 30 per cent of the distance. To make up for this he had attempted to stretch the cable by keeping it taut on the drums, and stringing it out so that it looped from peak to peak.

This arangement worked for a short time, but when the offshore currents began swinging and swaying the loops, they soon ground the cable through, causing expensive repair jobs.

When Major Field learned of Mitchell's plan to work through the winter, he said, "You'll never do it, Bill. You'll never get anyone up here to work during those months. It's asking too much of the men."

"Major, I'm going to put my part of the line through, if it takes me twenty years. I know we'll have some trouble, but it's the only way the job can be done. You watch us rig wire next summer!"

Lieutenant Mitchell's party moved on to Skagway where they waited for the interior to freeze up tight. The time was not wasted. Equipment was inspected and everyone learned to use snowshoes, drive dog teams, and take charge of the freight sleds. While his men remained at the base, organizing the loads of telegraph equipment and supplies, Bill went off with guides to survey the route the line would take. His sector was to run between Eagle City on the Yukon, south to Valdez on Prince William Sound.

Now the temperature had fallen to 48 degrees below zero, but the Yukon valley afforded endless vistas of majestic beauty. Large blocks of ice were already piled up, resembling great castles and redoubts. Here and there warm springs, repelling the cold, formed open areas from which great clouds of vapor drifted across the countryside to clear-varnish everything with a crystal plating.

Despite the cold, heavy clothing was out of the question. Old-timers had warned: "You can't expect to run a dog sled, and then stand around to rest. The sweat you'd generate would quickly freeze, and you'd not be able to move again."

This was one of the most important lessons Bill learned in that frozen wild. He knew that he would be making long, high-speed runs, so he chose a pair of Eskimo moccasins, heavy socks, mittens and the typical parka. Then he improvised a long, loose hunting shirt made of bed-ticking—a tightly woven fabric that would keep out the wind. This shirt had a fur-lined hood that protruded well beyond the face to protect the cheeks and nose from cross winds. A modern variation of bed-ticking is the Arctic cloth used by American forces in Alaska today.

Today our men at other sub-Arctic posts and at the South Pole are provided with a type of this fabric that is very light but wind resistant.

This rule of not risking high perspiration came to Bill's aid that winter. One day he had two dog teams on a surveying trip that took him over a waterway then known as Tokyo River. He had a companion named Emmett who was not too familiar with winter conditions, and neither one realized how treacherous a frozen river can be. On the surface it looked as if the ice must be many feet thick, but in this instance they crossed at a point where the pressure of river water had forced itself through wide cracks and had run on over the surface ice. That night this water had frozen over again, but was not thick enough to withstand the weight of a loaded sled.

Running in the lead, Billy hit one of these treacherous areas and crashed through—dog team, sled and all—into the icy water. His favorite lead dog, Pointer, got a toe hold on the splintered edge of ice, and loyal to his trust, hauled out the second dog. Bill, finding another layer of ice almost three feet below, worked his way forward and shoved the rest of the dogs clear.

Meanwhile, Emmett came tearing up, and his team and sled went through only a few yards from where Pointer and Bill were trying to get their gear free.

In his next letter home Bill told the story in some detail. It is easy to imagine the new melodramatic extravaganza the girls at Meadowmere put on.

"We were both completely soaked," Bill wrote, "and

the minute we crawled out of the water and tried to haul the sleds clear, we were frozen stiff. Our moccasins were as stiff as boards. This is what the old-timers meant by warning us never to allow our clothing to get damp, either from perspiration or careless sled-running.

"I sensed that if we did not act quickly we would be frozen to death in a few minutes. Already, we found it difficult to move. The handles of our axes, lashed to the top of the sleds, were covered in ice and difficult to get at. As we worked at the pack, I spotted a dry tree trunk leaning over the river's edge. Providence must have put it there for fools like us. Both Emmett and I turned the dogs and sleds toward this ancient trunk, and then we cut the dogs loose to give them a chance to shake themselves dry and warm. By this time I was completely stiff, so I jumped back into the water—to 'warm' off again. Imagine jumping into icy water to keep from freezing to death?

"In the meantime Emmett had unleashed an ax and I saw him take a hefty swipe at the dead tree. The ax broke in two, it was so brittle from the cold. Emmett stood there staring at this strange phenomenon, then I realized that he was freezing stiff too, so I ordered him into the water to become flexible again. With that, I took a second ax, and for a few strokes all went well, but finally that ax handle broke in the middle. I had a few chips started, and Emmett, somewhat free to move again, went to his sled and found a third ax. I hurried to my load and hauled out a small can of kerosene with the idea of starting a quick fire, but the kerosene was frozen. I began to lose hope, but somehow found the courage to jump back into the water again, during which time Emmett had the tree down and well splintered. Soon we had a small fire going.

"We both had to jump into the water once more, but we quickly had a roaring blaze. You should have seen us, shoving the dogs out of the glow and warmth to get our half-naked selves up close enough to dry out our clothing. When we found time to check on the temperature, our thermometer showed 60 degrees below zero!"

The surveys had to go on and provided many hair-raising adventures. One day Bill and his party mushed a distance of fifty miles to reach a settlement known as Fortymile. They were totally exhausted and the party holed up for the night, expecting to awake the next morning beaten and crippled by the long run. To Lieutenant Mitchell's amazement he discovered that everyone had withstood the ordeal magnificently, and he decided that the clear, cold weather afforded a restorative power never before experienced.

They rounded up the dogs after breakfast, snapped them into their harness, and started off again, hoping to repeat the previous day's performance. The trick to dog sledding is in knowing how to ride the sled when it is moving easily at a fast clip. On these carriers a small step had been fitted above one of the runners where the driver could "hook a ride" when the track was straight and level. It was steered by a gee pole, some six or eight feet in length, attached to the front end of the right runner. While running along or riding the step, the driver steered the sled with his gee pole, and in that manner kept it on the trail.

They made more than twenty-five miles before lunch, and about an hour later Mitchell's sled was stopped suddenly by a large drift-covered hole. The lieutenant was thrown forward hard, catching his knee against a large outcropping of ice. The impact almost knocked Bill out, and his leg stiffened up in a very short time. He feared that the kneecap was punctured and releasing the lubricating fluid that might freeze and leave him crippled for life.

Everyone moved fast. His companions rearranged one sled's cargo, laid Bill on it, and made him as comfortable as possible. Then, mushing on, they finally reached a cabin about ten miles ahead where one of the guides, Ben Tillman, started a fire before hurrying off to Fort Egbert. Another man, named Webb, stayed on to keep the fire going and to apply hot and cold applications until the knee's soreness was eased. The next day Tillman came back with a horse which Billy rode back to the fort.

This knee gave him considerable trouble all that winter, but Bill ignored it and worked on as though nothing had happened. He did not wish to be considered a light-duty soldier, and perhaps ordered back home. The injury annoyed him for years. Later in life he carried a cane, which many people thought was a dandy's affectation. Bill always laughed and admitted that it was, but actually he needed its support and it kept him going when many a man would have used the disability to quit the Army and claim a pension.

Bill rested at Fort Egbert, where he superintended the work of setting out the equipment and supplies for the telegraph line. He lived in a log hut, went out on a number of surveying trips as usual, but also found time to go hunting. On one trip he shot one hundred grouse in a day, providing a "poultry dinner" for every man on the base. At night he pored over his books and plans, and it was here that he developed his administrative ability. He soon had his share of the line planned out, and always knew where every man and every crate of supplies were located. He continued his military studies, but whenever he sorted over his few books, he always stopped at a slim volume on aeronautics and read about this new science night after night.

From Fort Egbert he wrote to his father, explaining that he was certain the Army would be his career, but realized that if he wished to reach the top, he would have to get out of the Signal Corps. By this time the early reports of Marconi's new wireless system indicated that the telegraph wire would soon be replaced. He sensed that he would have either to delve deeper into the wireless instrument, or make plans to enter another branch of the service.

He made no particular reference to aviation, but what had been accomplished in Europe and the United States held him enthralled. He read that captive balloons had been manned for high-level scouting in the

Civil War. Balloons had played an important role in the 1870 Siege of Paris. Sixty-eight of them had been used to get important personages and messages out beyond the siege lines. The French had flown four war balloons against the Chinese during the battle of Hoang-Ho, outside Tonkin in present-day Vietnam. Fascinating experiments, involving powered model aircraft and man-carrying gliders, were being reported regularly. Sir Hiram Maxim had designed and built a steam-powered airplane that flew along a wooden track. Men were working on cycle-powered planes, and weird contrivances that were intended to fly were being constructed in many countries. It was obvious to Bill Mitchell that someone soon would uncover the secret of powered flight.

It was just a matter of time.

Bill left Fort Egbert in January 1902, with two men, dog teams and camping outfits. He planned to be out for the rest of the winter. He would do his own surveying with a prismatic compass and lay out the final trail for his line across country. He had arranged that forty-two of his men, driving thirty mules, were to follow.

In laying out the work, Bill had decided on the cache system, in which all equipment was to be moved out from the main base at once, and men and supplies dropped off each night, with the rest of the train going on. In this manner tons of equipment could be distributed in a short time; and time was most important.

The civilian labor which he had recruited to drive

the supply teams was composed of a lot of unruly sourdoughs, mule skinners, packing-plant workers or loaf-
ers, who usually holed up for the winter and spent their
hard-earned money on drink and gambling. A number
of them, who regretted having signed on for this sub-
zero job, began an undercover plan to delay the whole
operation. They were certain that they would not live
through that winter.

Lieutenant Mitchell learned of this revolt and noted
the early slackness in making up the sled loads. He
decided to take a strong hand. He reminded them that
they had signed work contracts, and then he arranged
that each sled would have an armed soldier as well as
a civilian driver.

This new discipline kept the group together for a
short time, until the sled train was moving off for the
bank of the Yukon River. Then, with a signal from
their ringleader, all but four of the civilians deserted
the sleds and refused to move off into the frozen night.

"All right," Lieutenant Mitchell said, accepting the
situation. "You'll get your due pay, but you'll never
get another government job as long as I am in Alaska.
I want every one of you off this post in half an hour."

Bill then went back to town and recruited another
group, offering them double the original pay, and in
this way finally signed on a crew he could depend on.

Their objective was the Fortymile post down the
Yukon, and in spite of weather, cold and rugged going,
the party covered an average of twenty miles a day.
At the end of each day they dropped off a cache of supplies, two men and a dog team. Bill went ahead, select-

ing the best route, seldom bothering with a tent, but making the most of what could be found on the trail. His enthusiasm was inspiring and the men worked like demons trying to keep pace with him. Within a few days they even seemed to enjoy the work.

Thompson Pass has one of the greatest snowfalls anywhere in the world, and when Mitchell's party breasted it, there were eighty-five feet of snow to be negotiated. So Bill waited until spring when the soft snow had melted away and a new, secure trail could be made by having his men and sleds pack it down. There were times when the mules broke through in areas of warm springs, and their feet froze. When bits were put into the horses' mouths, their jaws were frostbitten and broke out in sores. Many of these animals had to be shot, but the work continued.

A group of Signal Corps men came on behind the fast-moving Mitchell party and strung wire over the frozen ground. They tested it out with buzzer instruments and found the cold to be a great insulator. They were confident now that the line would go through— and work.

At the same time, another line crew was working north from Valdez, and it was hoped that both parties would meet halfway. But Bill's group, working under the lieutenant's lash of enthusiasm, was first at the meeting point.

Once the winter work of distributing the equipment and supplies was over, the actual erection of the poles and line the next summer was comparatively easy. Mitchell had strung his section of 125 miles, carrying his survey lines along the Good Pasture River and across a country that had never been trodden by the foot of a white man. The line was completed well within the two-year period that Bill had predicted.

His 1902 report included the following: "We made it, but the toil and hardships experienced cannot be fully appreciated by anyone unfamiliar with Alaskan trails. Suffice it to say that every pound of food, forage, tentage, wire, insulators or line materials had to be moved by pack animals over a trail so rough that an animal can hardly travel fifteen miles a day.

"Cold and rapid glacial streams, swampy morasses, tangled underbrush, steep declivities, narrow canyons, thick timber and sharp ridges alternate to tax the strength of man and animal to the upmost. The monotony of the life is exceedingly trying, after the novelty of the scenery disappears. Rarely is any large game or even birdlife seen, and humanity, whether in the shape of a prospector or Indian, appears infrequently. When to these conditions are added the physical discomforts attendant on frequent falls of rain in summer and snow in winter, with high, cutting winds, it requires a firmness of purpose to persevere to the end.

"In closing, it is doubted whether in the peaceful annals of the Army equal conditions of hardship and privation have been met with nobler fortitude by enlisted men."

Lieutenant Mitchell was developing a beautiful command of the English language, as well as broad experience in administration and adventure.

Chapter 6

I WANT TO FLY

In RECOGNITION of his work in helping to build the telegraph network linking the new American territory with Washington, Lieutenant William Mitchell was promoted to captain. He left Alaska in July, 1903, and was transferred to a new post in Denver, Colorado. There, and later on at Fort Leavenworth in Kansas, he pursued the study of military telegraphy. He was also interested in fitting the automobile into service transport, and was among the first military men in the United States to realize the value of the photographic camera for reconnaissance work.

It should be pointed out that Mitchell was still the patrician type of soldier. Few young men on his social level considered making the Army a career. In some respects, having a fortune behind him was a great help, in others it was a serious handicap and sometimes got him into trouble. As he rose to authority, his out-

spokenness and resounding views annoyed his superiors.
He reasoned: Someone has to explain to the armchair
generals what is going on. Most younger officers wish
to, but don't dare risk their jobs. With me, I don't care.
I can always go back and work at Meadowmere or in
one of my father's banks. I'm the one who should speak
up.

He was only twenty-three, but his months of experience in Cuba, the Philippines and Alaska had given
him a firm grip on many military subjects. He had
traveled through the Far East and was to visit the
battlefields of the Russo-Japanese War. When he married Caroline Stoddard of Rochester, New York, he
spent his honeymoon in the Caribbean, chiefly to consider American defenses in Mexico and Cuba. Later he
took his bride on a tour through the Southern states
and at one time left her, to participate in the first large-
scale military maneuvers since the Civil War.

It is difficult to picture Billy Mitchell as an emo-
tional and romantic bridegroom, for he was too involved with his own imaginings. He puzzled over the
new Marconi wireless telegraph, he delved into the
history of rockets and kite balloons and the possibility
of aerial photography. On one occasion during field
maneuvers Mitchell used a fast motorcar—the first ever
used by American forces—and built a tall tower on a
hill from which to spy on the enemy while they were
deploying for action. His side quickly overwhelmed
the opposition and the referees had to call off the
maneuver, rule out Mitchell's tall tower and high-speed

automobile for dispatch carrying, and start again. This was the sort of frustration Bill encountered all his military life.

But he was so engrossed in the many variations of his service life, he almost missed the greatest event in the world's aeronautical history. On December 17, 1903, the Wright Brothers made their first successful heavier-than-air flight, a hop of just fifty-nine seconds. Young Mitchell and his bride were honeymooning in Mexico, and since the feat received little attention in the American press at the time—even the Wrights' home-town paper, the Dayton *Journal* refused to print such a fantastic story—it is quite possible nothing was known of the event for many months. Not until two years later, when the Wright Brothers were flying daily from a farmer's pasture near Dayton, was particular notice taken of the two bicycle repairmen and their noisy contraption.

Many historians have created the impression that Billy Mitchell was one of our earliest pilots, that he was trained by the Wright Brothers, and that he was one of the first U. S. Army pilots. Such was not the case. From the time he returned from Alaska, he was deeply engrossed in advancing all types of Signal Corps work. He was concerned with the improvement of the kite balloon, the development of aerial observation and the training of men for this kind of work. It was some time before the airplane was considered seriously as Signal Corps equipment.

In his particular field Bill came in contact with the

progress of Zeppelin-type dirigibles, and learned that some European experts were suggesting the Zeppelin could be used for reconnaissance, troop transport and even certain strategic exercises.

He once commented: "One of these dirigibles could fly over a battlefield, carry messages out of a besieged fortress, and by towing a balloon loaded with explosive could drop bombs in the midst of the enemy's fortifications."

"Why a towed balloon?" someone inquired.

"It would have to be done that way," Mitchell explained, "since no one has figured out how to compensate for the dropping of a pound or two of load, which would allow the dirigible to rise so fast its envelope would crack."

This amusing explanation apparently reassured many conservative military men that no enemy dirigible would ever fly over and drop bombs on America. Mitchell warned them, however, that Zeppelins could fly over the ocean at several hundred feet, act as scouts for the Navy, and "detect" the presence of submarine vessels.

On August 1, 1907, an Aeronautical Division was organized within the Signal Corps, indicating that the airplane had been accepted as a unit of military value. At the time Billy had no connection with this branch because he was a married man and thus ineligible for flight training. Airplane flying was thought to be too risky for the heads of families, and so far as we know, Billy made no real effort to break the rule.

He was most engrossed in a book, published in 1904, entitled *The Military Policy of the United States,* written by General Emory Upton. The general advocated a complete modernization of the Army, and the use of the Continental Plan—one based on universal conscription. This idea was pushed further by Elihu Root, President Theodore Roosevelt's Secretary of War.

Mitchell was serving as a student in a year-long course of the Army School of the Line. He had been permitted to stay on for a second year to take the Staff College course, where General Upton's book was contributing a wealth of information and instruction. A major research problem was assigned to Bill and a group of his fellow officers, and everyone concerned realized that in the event of a major conflict, the United States was no better than a second-rate military power when compared with the armies and navies being established by many European nations—and Japan.

In those days Americans believed that the Atlantic and Pacific Oceans were too great a barrier for any European or Asian force to break through. How could fleets of battleships steam three or four thousand miles, attack our coastline, and then unload great armies to invade our important cities? It was impossible; they might get here, but with the coaling problems how would they get back?

Only men like Billy Mitchell who had served in the outposts realized just how these invasions could be carried out. They knew the value of small islands, coaling stations and jump-off points. We had assumed the obligation of defending the Philippines and Hawaii. We were most interested in Korean, Manchurian and Chinese trade—a point both China and Japan resented.

As a matter of fact, Captain Mitchell stated openly: "Increasing friction between Japan and the United States will take place in the future, and this will eventually lead to war."

But America was not interested in Japan—or Europe. We were spreading out, pushing the frontier farther West. Railroads were linking up new cities, and our natural resources seemed unending. We went through periods of prosperity, financial panic and varied disasters, but we said, "We're a new country, and we have to learn this way. But we want no war. We have had enough war. Let those who want these conflicts keep them to themselves—or fight on their own."

All these problems, theories and study occupied the young captain between 1904 and 1913. In 1912 he was appointed to a three-year tour on the General Staff at Washington, the youngest officer ever given such a post. He was then thirty-two.

In August, 1914, war broke out in Europe. By that time General Upton's Continental Army Plan had been accepted generally, and was known as the Preparedness Movement. Billy Mitchell was in his element, writing articles for magazines and newspapers pointing out the practicality of the plan. He argued that any objection to it was impractical idealism, the result of so many years of peace. He also explained that the advances in military science, particularly in transport methods, had brought us closer to our possible enemies, and that distance could no longer be measured in miles, but in time.

While the European War was presenting the threat of the submarine, the use of poison gas, trench warfare, mass bombardment, air attacks by airplanes and dirigibles and a full-scale war in the air, the United States ignored the many new weapons, the size of artillery, the speed and range of military aircraft and the advanced methods of war. The European conflict was 3,000 miles away, and even when a German cargo submarine arose from the depths of the Atlantic Ocean and tied up in an American port, no one seemed to realize the threat.

But by April, 1917, German aggressiveness and refusal to observe the rights of neutral nations forced us into the fray. Although we had had thirty-three months in which to watch and observe the progress of the War, we had made no practical preparation.

Captain Mitchell, contemplating the situation, realized that when we were forced into the conflict we would require a great Army, a Navy, and an Air Service. His keen mind knew that it would take a new system of management to handle these huge forces. Money would not matter particularly, but if men and money were to be contributed in fantastic figures, it would need a sharp, orderly mind and complete Federal control to keep them in hand.

Bill spent many months developing this theme. The managerial role fascinated him, and during this period of his career he found out how far he could go, if given the chance. We can see why Billy Mitchell fought for strong, efficient forces and how, later, he became so obsessed with this great ambition that he failed to keep his enthusiasm within bounds—because he could afford to take the risk.

This was when Billy began to make his first mistakes. They were not serious errors, but in his enthusiasm and eagerness to get his views into print, he often made avoidable blunders. For instance, as a Signal Corps representative on the General Staff he came into contact with matters concerning his aviation section. His interest in the airplane, despite its use in European forces, was somewhat detached, and he once said: "Aviation is at best a reconnaissance device; hence it is or should be an integral part of the Signal Corps communication system. The offensive value of the airplane has yet to be proved. Experiments are being carried out with bomb-dropping, and some machines have been fitted with guns, but we can only consider these experiments."

Wiser heads than Bill's had been saying much the same thing for years, so he can be forgiven for this lack of foresight. But to read that he had once objected strenuously to putting aviation into a separate branch, shows that he was not always convinced of the value of air power. (Later on, Congress changed the title of the Aeronautical Division to that of the Aviation Section, and brought minor improvements in the status of the personnel and equipment.)

Meanwhile the war in Europe thundered on. Airplanes were now dropping bombs and carrying machine guns. Pilots were becoming world-renowned for their abilities to shoot down enemy airplanes. The flying boat was having an important role in naval affairs. For their own protection and to make the most of their gunpower, airplanes were flying in definite formations. A few American volunteer fliers were with the French Air Service, and hundreds more were enlisting with the British.

Late in 1915, Billy Mitchell was given the task of preparing a survey of American aviation needs. In his report he theorized that aviation would be a particularly valuable adjunct to the Army, "the second line of defense," in the event that the Navy, "the first line of defense," should fail to stop an invading enemy. He added that, attached to harbor and mobile coast defenses within the Continental United States and our overseas possessions, aviation would be useful for reconnaissance, for preventing hostile aerial reconnaissance, for destroying hostile aircraft and in offensive work against enemy submarines and other vessels. Aviation would also aid in spotting the fire of coastal artillery, both against ships and against any invading force that might invest the seacoast fortifications.

This report was considered important enough to be put out in pamphlet form. But even Mitchell's most ardent admirers had to admit that all this, and much

more, was already being done with aviation in the
European War. As a result, however, Billy suddenly
found himself the chief spokesman for the Aviation
Service. The report induced Congress to provide an
airplane detachment to back up Pershing's Mexican
Border campaign, and more important, alerted the
American public to the seriousness of the situation.

Now a thirty-six-year-old major, Mitchell discovered
that he was a nonflying hero of the Aviation Service,
but because of his status and age could not be given
Army flight training. In order to remedy this, Bill, who
was to become one of America's best-known military
pilots, paid out $1,470 from his own pocket to the
Curtiss School at Newport News, Virginia. He made
thirty-six instruction flights and had almost twenty-five
hours of flying time before he was considered a proficient pilot.

This training was not easy to gain, since he was busy
in Washington all week and had only Sundays free. He
used to take a boat down the Potomac River and get
off at Newport News on Saturday night. He would fly
as much as possible all the next day, and hurry back to
his office by Monday morning. After four days of dual-
control instruction under his teacher, Walter Lees,
Bill made his first solo flight. From all accounts, he was
hardly ready, for he cracked up the trainer plane in a
bad landing. He admitted later, "That mishap taught
me more about flying than all the words of my instructor."

By March, 1917, the Comptroller of the Treasury

ruled that, although officers in Mitchell's category could now fly military airplanes, the present statutes provided no funds for training taken at civilian schools. This mattered little to Bill, for he was assured of an active aviation career, and as a man who had proven himself an administrator and was now a flyer, he enjoyed the respect of both his superiors and juniors.

Once he had the support of everyone in the Aviation Section, Bill set to work to enlarge his air force, and laid ambitious plans for its future expansion. Congress appropriated a sum of $13,000,000 for aviation—although no one knew where this money was to be spent —and President Wilson authorized the creation of an aerial-reserve corps of 500 pilots. But there were no government facilities to train these men, so Mitchell broke the log jam by making arrangements with civilian schools to train pilots at government expense. When he saw what was being done in Europe, Major Mitchell started a nation-wide campaign to enroll men between the ages of twenty-one and twenty-seven (with a college education, or its equivalent) in these flying courses.

The spring of 1917 marked a new page of destiny for Billy Mitchell. America now realized there was no escaping her responsibility as a world power. President Wilson had been re-elected to office on the slogan, HE KEPT US OUT OF WAR, but many military men knew that war was inevitable.

While America hesitated, Billy realized that she had nothing but manpower and industrial potential with

which to fight, and secured an assignment from the
War Department to go to Europe as a military observer. A week after his arrival abroad America entered
the conflict. Here we see that a man, one of the few
fitted for the job, was at the front when air power had
passed through its embryo stages and had become a full-
fledged military arm.

This was not a period of wartime crates and ragtime
pilots flying Curtiss Jennies, as so many postwar historians and movie-scenario writers have depicted. The
aircraft were beautifully built machines, powered with
the finest of engines. The term "crate" is relative, and
the airplanes employed by both sides were tremendous
improvements over the equipment used at the outbreak of war in 1914.

The enemy had squadrons of first-class Albatros
fighters, two-seater fighters and armed multiplace aircraft for trench strafing. The British had produced the
Bristol Fighter, probably the finest warplane of the
campaign. They also had the famed Sopwith Camel,
which destroyed more enemy aircraft than any fighter
before or since. Their S.E.5 was almost indestructible.
They had six-gun fighters coming down the assembly
lines, and a new fleet of long-range bombers was getting
its first trial flights. The French were having great success with the gadfly Nieuport, while their sturdy Spad
was the war horse of dozens of new fighter squadrons.
Ace pilots—men with five or more enemy planes to
their credit—were writing amazing combat stories in

the skies. Never in all history had such glamorous performers played before such an audience.

When he got to the French front, Bill could not believe his eyes. There were airplanes he had never conceived of, and missions were being carried out that had
never occurred to him. His meager training in no way
fitted him to fly any of these warplanes. He had to get
French and British pilots to give him instruction and
eventually check him out on high-speed equipment. To
his credit, he soon learned. He flew on observation
patrols as an observer gunner. He went up in kite balloons and watched the observers carry out artillery
"shoots," directing the fire of the ground guns while
scouting the target from their balloon baskets. Week
after week he raced from one battle front to the other,
regardless of the risk, in order to absorb as much campaign knowledge as possible.

For his interest and willingness to share their many
hazards, the French awarded him the Croix de Guerre.

Chapter 7

WAR IN THE AIR

WITHIN three weeks Major William Mitchell had become the most popular of the American heroes on the Front. He was the first United States Army flyer to cross the enemy lines, and he had already been decorated for his courage. Making the most of his popularity, with the aid of several French officers Bill drew up a preliminary plan for the creation of an American air force; one that he hoped would go into action by the autumn of 1917. It called for a total of 5,000 airplanes by May 1, 1918, to be serviced by 38,500 mechanics.

Bill artfully had the project presented to Washington by Premier Ribot of France. The Premier, using Major Mitchell's own words, suggested that the United States plan to train 5,000 pilots, and make arrangements to turn out 2,000 planes and 4,000 engines a month. At that time the American air arm consisted of 52 officers and 1,100 men, plus about 200 civilian mechanics. Of a total of 130 so-called pilots, only 26 were qualified to fly any of the 55 serviceable aircraft, none of which was considered combat type.

Bill remained in France, continuing his study of the situation. He rented an expensive suite of rooms at the Hôtel Crillon in Paris and called in every available American, military or civilian, to help him set up an unauthorized Aviation Section Headquarters. He fully believed that within a month or two he would have hundreds of Americans enrolled in French aviation schools, and boasted that by late July America would put six squadrons on the line.

While all this was being planned, Billy rounded out his own flight training at Le Bourget airfield, under a French instructor, Victor Furmat.

Early in June, Bill sensed a slowdown in aviation power-plant production, and suggested to the War Department that American factories undertake the manufacture of several successful French and British engines. But he had no luck. Back home a manufacturing project had been started to produce what was known as the Liberty engine. This program gained great renown in the headlines of the day, but failed to produce a worth-while engine.

In the meantime some effort was made to deliver U.S. ground troops to the front, with General John J. Pershing arriving in Paris to head up the American effort. Bill was promoted to lieutenant colonel so that he might serve as the ranking aviation officer on Pershing's staff. This was how matters were planned, but new air missions of "experts" were being sent over from Washington, to clutter the French and British establishments.

Being busy, Colonel Mitchell seldom knew of these other groups until he was told of their arrival by his French comrades. By July 4, when the first American division to reach France paraded before General Pershing, Marshal Joffre of France and other military officials, Bill noted: "Our air force consists of one Nieuport plane which I use myself—and that is all."

While on a tour of the Front one day with Major Armengaud of the French General Staff, Colonel Mitchell's fast Mercedes broke down. Another car that was following, with Major T. F. Dodd who had also been assigned to Pershing's staff as an aviation official, pulled up behind. Dodd's chauffeur hopped out, lifted the Mercedes' hood, and soon found the trouble. Bill was impressed by the man's skill and asked who he was.

"That's Eddie Rickenbacker, one of the Indianapolis track drivers. He's been with Pershing's party for a couple of weeks."

"Seems like a good man."

Eddie Rickenbacker had long desired to get into the Aviation Service. When Bill heard of this he made things easy and persuaded General Pershing to relinquish his chauffeur to the flying service. The choice turned out well for all concerned. Eddie Rickenbacker became America's ace of aces, with twenty-six victories to his credit.

John Lendrum Mitchell, Jr., Bill's youthful brother,

joined the Air Service around the same time. He was thirteen years younger than the lieutenant colonel, and a graduate of the University of Wisconsin, where he had studied engineering. There were volunteers aplenty, but no aircraft. Instead there was a constant reshuffling of commanding officers, and Billy became impatient with the manner in which the project was being handled. Possibly to keep him quiet, he was raised to the rank of full colonel and made chief of the air forces in the Zone of Advance, where he hoped his first squadrons would see action.

American stay-at-home officials continued to boast about what we were doing in this War. The House Military Affairs Committee was told that during the first half of 1918 the country would produce 12,000 airplanes and 24,000 engines. In October, 1917, Secretary of War, Newton D. Baker, proclaimed that 20,000 planes were then under construction; something of an exaggeration. Other less reliable sources were making even wilder boasts. This was not only unfair to the American public and our Allies, but these fantastic reports whipped the Germans into greater efforts. They immediately enlarged their industrial and manufacturing facilities. When April 1918 rolled around, we still did not have an American squadron on the front. The enemy had twice as many as they would have had, without our advance warning.

Although Colonel Mitchell was building up valued relations with the British and French, General Pershing realized that matters were not running smoothly in the new U.S. Air Service. Billy's kite balloons worked very well with the artillery and in furnishing limited-range reconnaissance, but the lack of aircraft meant that the French had to provide air cover and support. This created humiliating situations. Pershing probably felt that Colonel Mitchell was of more use in the active areas and that administrative work should be in the hands of a less excitable man.

It was at this point that the Secretary of War appointed General Benjamin Foulois to go over and take charge of all American aviation in France. As was to be expected, Mitchell and Foulois were soon at loggerheads, so General Pershing appointed General Mason M. Patrick of the Corps of Engineers to head up the whole American Air Service.

General Foulois was given command of the Air Force Services of Supply and Schools in the rear areas, and Mitchell, who became a brigadier general late in 1918, was placed in charge of all fighting squadrons at the front.

When by March 15, 1918, only one American-built *DH-4* had arrived in France, Billy went to see Pershing and a hot argument resulted. The general told him that if he did not stop trying to change the organization of the Air Service, he would send him home.

"You do that, sir," Colonel Mitchell raged, "and I'll bet you'll soon follow me!"

There was no answer to that. Pershing burst out

laughing. The argument closed on a more convivial note.

After the long-remembered German "push" in March 1918, Mitchell somehow "borrowed" airfields, hangars and a few French aircraft and finally proclaimed America's entry into the air war. This came on Sunday April 14, 1918—practically one year after the declaration of war by the United States. The first fighter patrol went over the line to intercept enemy planes, and Lieutenants Douglas Campbell and Alan Winslow each shot down a German aircraft. Fortunately, both machines fell inside the French lines and the pilots were captured. It was America's first victory, the baptism of fire for Mitchell's air force, and the news heartened the French and American publics tremendously.

This opening success was followed in short order by other American victories, and in a few weeks American names, such as Hartney, Campbell, Rickenbacker and Meissner were emblazoned on the Allied ace list. Billy Mitchell was greatly encouraged by the showing his boys were making, flying second-rate aircraft loaned by the French.

There were setbacks and defeats, to be sure. On May 19, Raoul Lufbery, a Connecticut lad who had been flying for the French in the Lafayette Escadrille, was shot down during his first combat patrol as an American Air Service flyer. Like so many more, Lufbery had been induced to transfer into the U.S. service, and had been sitting around with nothing to do as he awaited the formation of an all-American squadron. This layoff had probably dulled the edge of his skill, for although he had shot down seventeen enemy aircraft, he was completely outclassed by a German airman flying a new Albatros.

Hearing of this intrusion of the enemy plane over his sector, Billy had raced out to his own Nieuport, hoping to get into the air in time to intercept the Albatros. But Lufbery had already taken off, and Mitchell had to stand on the field and watch his most experienced pilot go down to defeat. The enemy airman was skilled and daring, and in a short time had put a telling burst into Lufbery's fuselage. Tracer bullets pierced his gasoline tank, and in a few seconds the plane burst into flames.

Raoul Lufbery had always spoken of his dread of fire in the air, and had said that if it ever happened to him he would take the easy way out—jump. The Allied pilots had no parachutes in those days, although the Germans had long experimented with a seat-pack type. One or two of their noted airmen had been saved by these chutes. But Raoul had little choice, and he fell in the flower garden of an old shoe cobbler's cottage.

This loss affected Billy Mitchell more than he would admit at the time. He made immediate inquiry into the possibility of providing parachutes for his flyers. But, strange to relate, this idea was ridiculed—not by the nonflying Top Brass—but by the pilots themselves!

At that time few flyers had any idea that a parachute could be designed to afford complete safety and yet be compact enough to fit into the confined cockpits of that day. The parachutes that were supplied to our observers in the kite balloons were bulky affairs, carried in large, conical, leather containers hung over the sides of the baskets. It was these devices that most pilots visualized whenever the subject of parachutes came up.

On May 26 Colonel Mitchell suffered another deep loss. While having luncheon in a café in Toul, his aide, Captain Kelleher, came up to his table and said, "I'm afraid I have some bad news, sir."

Billy pushed back his chair.

"Your brother John has crashed."

"Is he dead?"

"He was coming in at Colombey-les-Belles when his plane apparently broke up. He was killed instantly."

This time Billy took a week off to make sure that John would get a proper burial, and at the first opportunity he had a photograph taken of the grave and sent home to their mother.

Although he flew over the line at least once every day, mainly to keep track of his squadrons and to learn how the ground war was progressing, he nevertheless continued to consult with other air leaders and keep in touch with everything going on at every front.

General Hugh Trenchard, who had built up the British Royal Flying Corps to one of the most powerful forces in the War, became Billy's firm friend. He welcomed the American leader whenever he dropped in at the R.F.C. Headquarters, and willingly shared his

views and future plans. On one occasion Bill was taken
on a tour of inspection, and realized that "Boom"
Trenchard was a man not bound by traditions. He was
years ahead of his time. He was planning underground
hangars to protect his aircraft, and his views on the
future of aviation held Bill spellbound.

After several flights over the shell-battered British
front with General C. A. H. Longcroft, one of Trenchard's top men, at the controls, it was pointed out that
at the rate the ground armies were going it would take
months to cross the no man's land that separated the
British from the enemy. When he returned from one
of the flights, Trenchard entrusted Billy with a confidential paper in which he had outlined his ideas of air
power and how it should be used.

In general, General Trenchard's views ran: "The
airplane is an offensive weapon, not a defensive
weapon. As a weapon of attack, the airplane cannot be
estimated too highly. Air power, properly organized,
will make it possible to attack and continue to attack,
even though the enemy is on the offensive. Aviation can
stop ground attacks, break up transport and communications, but, more important, let us presume that the
Ruhr district around Essen, the arsenal of the enemy
powers, could be destroyed by air bombers. It would be
a terrible blow to Germany. We have been using the
airplane improperly. No amount of flying machines can
prevent an enemy aircraft from crossing the lines. The
sky itself is too large to defend. We must plan military
aviation to attack the rear areas of any enemy and

destroy all means of supply. Because of this, air power will one day become much more important than sea power."

When Mitchell left the British front to return to Paris, he read and reread General Trenchard's confidential paper. Now he was more than ever determined to build up America's air power to meet the specifications the big, burly Britisher had outlined.

Just before the war ended, Billy went to Pershing with the most advanced idea of air-infantry co-operation. He was determined to capture Metz, an important city not too far inside the German lines. He proposed to use sixty squadrons of British Handley-Page bombers, each squadron to consist of twenty twin-engined aircraft, and fill them with one of America's crack infantry divisions. He did not explain where they were to get these aircraft. General "Boom" Trenchard also had requirements for the big bombers, but he was never able to raise more than one squadron.

However, Billy Mitchell was working on the airborne infantry idea as early as 1918. His 12,000-man force was to be flown across the lines, fitted with non-existent parachutes, and dropped into the German area —to take Metz. His plan was well thought out and probably would have worked. But the Germans, realizing that their War was lost, capitulated before the Handley-Pages could be built, or infantry troops trained in parachute operations.

Chapter 8

VICTORY IN THE AIR

Despite the late start, and the failure of American industry to provide suitable aircraft, Billy Mitchell's flyers contributed greatly to the Allied victory. By midsummer of 1918 we had many first-class squadrons on the front, all doing valuable work, all combining to drive the enemy back across the Rhine.

As soon as he was able, and with considerable help from the French, Mitchell set up a force of 1,500 airplanes which he used in mass strikes during the battle for the Saint-Mihiel salient that began on September 12. This succeeded in limiting enemy reconnaissance, and at the same time gained important information necessary for the ground forces to move ahead.

Over the next two days, Billy carried out his war as he had always wished; his pursuit planes battered at enemy fighter formations, his bombers saturated enemy back areas, and prevented any fast movement of troops or supplies. Sometimes bad weather interrupted this plan, but by now the whole Allied world knew that the Americans had learned how to fight this new type of war. It is noticeable that Mitchell's new success coincided with a general Allied advance from one end of the front to the other.

During the Meuse-Argonne offensive, which opened on September 26, Colonel Mitchell again showed his aviation skill and air-power handling. More than 600 American airplanes were integrated into the attack. Once more, great formations of bombers, escorted by fighters, ranged deep into enemy territory, broke the German supply lines, entangled their transport, and cut all-important communications. Enemy balloons were shot down by the dozens. We suffered great losses, but inflicted equal damage, and by now the end was in sight. When it was all over, Brigadier General William Mitchell could present a noteworthy report.

By November 11, 1918, there were 740 American-flown aircraft on the front, or about 10 per cent of the total aircraft strength of the Allies. Our bombers had carried out 150 separate bombing attacks, in which 138 tons of bombs had been dropped. Some of our airmen had penetrated as far as 160 miles behind the enemy lines. American losses in combat amounted to 289 planes and 48 balloons, and of this number 57 were aircraft piloted by American officers who flew with the British, French and Italians. American pilots had claimed 781 enemy planes and 73 kite balloons shot down. Mitchell's fighter squadrons boasted of 71 pilots who qualified as aces. This gallant company shot down 450 aircraft and 50 kite balloons.

In the closing days of the War Brigadier General William Mitchell was more renowned than General Pershing or Admiral Sims. He had proved himself, and the minute the Armistice was signed, he became one of the most flamboyant figures in the battle area. He designed his own uniforms. Forsaking the high-collar blouse of the American forces, he copied the flashiest of the French and British. His jacket had bellowed patch pockets, and he strode about in gaudy Bedford-cord breeches, swinging his famous cane like a swagger stick. He often appeared wearing every deco-ration and campaign medal that had been awarded him, when strict military tradition ruled that only the ribbons should be worn on active-service dress. But Billy Mitchell could do no wrong.

Sitting at the wheel of his roaring Mercedes, he raced from one big city to another, always the center of an admiring throng of British, French or American air-men. Although the war was over, he continued to bellow his belief in air power—sometimes in excited French, and when he ran out of that language, he rattled on in English. Billy felt, as did "Boom" Tren-chard, that he had been robbed of his greatest triumph. These two confidants, as unalike as two human beings could be, had been determined to blast to rubble every important manufacturing city in Germany.

Many other high-ranking officers in the American Air Service soon realized that although the European war was over, a new, and possibly more bitter, conflict was being prepared in Washington. A new Chief of Staff would soon replace General Pershing, and whoever was named to the post would no doubt bring his own personal staff to the War Department. They would all be officers from the ground forces. The Air Service would find itself left out again. This point was presented to Billy Mitchell, and many of his friends advised him to rush back home as quickly as possible.

Colonel "Hap" Arnold, who was to head America's Air Force in World War II, was insistent that Billy go back to Washington and there make the most of his War record if he hoped to become the new air chief. There was no one else who could hold such a job and keep the Air Service together. But for some strange reason, Mitchell refused, and instead decided to go to Germany with the Army of Occupation. He apparently wanted to drive his Mercedes in triumph down Berlin's Unter den Linden.

Germany had capitulated, but there was no actual military victory. This was a political surrender and the enemy was to repeat this point over and over in the years ahead. General Mitchell, like so many others, realized that the German Army had not been defeated. It had simply stopped fighting when it became obvious that victory was out of the question. The myth of the invincibility of German arms had not been destroyed, and all serious-thinking men knew that as long as the myth remained there would be no real peace in Europe.

But what was worse, this capitulation had robbed the Allies of their chance to prove the full value of their Air Services.

With all this in mind Billy Mitchell returned to the United States early in 1919, in the belief that he was to head up the peacetime Air Service. However, America was tired of war, and any plans for improving the military forces received little support. Soldiers, sailors and airmen were rushed home and demobilized as fast as the processing machinery would allow. Henry Ford was putting out a new cheap automobile, known affectionately as the "tin Lizzie." It was a car that could be bought for $500, and practically every returning service man who could rake together $500 bought one—and went off for the vacation he had dreamed of for nearly two long years.

Who cared whether the American Air Service was built up to suitable peacetime specifications?

When Mitchell returned home to this nationwide situation, he was aghast. Worse still, he learned that Major General C. T. Menoher, a former commander of the 42nd—Rainbow—Division and a gallant soldier with no aviation experience at all, had been appointed Chief of the Air Service. Naturally, Billy was disappointed but he continued his drive to improve the air arm. He feuded with General Menoher while he drilled new pilots and new squadron commanders, to keep them on their toes. The rags and tatters of what had once been a first-class Air Service on the Western Front, had been brought home, and the handful of staff officers who were still interested did their best to "keep 'em flying."

But there was no money and very few aircraft. Out on the West Coast one group organized a Forest Fire Patrol. A handful more, including Lieutenant James H. Doolittle, got together in the hope of doing research and development to improve engines and aircraft. Billy made an attempt to organize a transcontinental air race to stimulate interest in aviation in general.

There were no air lines in those days. Air mail was being carried over pathetic little five-mile hops from Long Island to New York City. A few war-weary *DH-4*s were loaded with small bags of mail, but it was a token effort at best and added little to the efficiency of the Post Office Department.

Only Billy Mitchell, it would seem, had the foresight to predict that one day people would fly aboard aircraft from city to city, and that a letter would be flown from New York to San Francisco in less than a day. He also was loud in his demands for a network of military air bases to be set up all over the country. But that took money, and America was not spending money on military aviation. "Sure, I'll fly," the jokers cracked, "if you'll let me keep one foot on the ground."

Although his country refused to buy him planes or build new airfields, Billy Mitchell was not stopped from preaching the doctrine of air power. He was no longer the gay, debonair war hero with rows of medals and gaudy uniforms. He was too busy writing articles for newspapers and aviation magazines. He resented

the fact that what money was available was being split
three ways; for the Army, Navy and Air Service. It
was in commenting on this that Billy made his big
mistake.

"What does the Navy need this money for?" he
asked. "Don't these entrenched admirals realize that
sea power is done for? One airplane, one bomb and we
can send the battleships to the bottom as fast as they
can be built. The money going into surface ships is
being wasted. For what it costs to build a dreadnought
we can build a whole wing of bombers. Nothing can
stand up to the modern bomber!"

This was all very well, and today we can see Billy
Mitchell's point. But back in the summer of 1919 he
had no bombers, and as for the bombs, nothing much
larger than a 500-pound missile had been carried any
distance and dropped with accuracy. The Navy could
argue that Britain and America had bottled up the
German Navy with no trouble at all. The Navy destroyers and Navy flying boats had frustrated the early
U-boats. No one could say that the Navy, with its
battleships and other surface vessels, hadn't held up its
end in the War. The Battle of Jutland might be a con-
troversial conflict, but the fact remained that the Germans had been driven back to Kiel and had not come
out again. Aircraft had had nothing to do with that.
Aircraft, the Navy men pointed out, had been too busy
shooting each other down.

Frustrated at every move, Billy turned to forming a
Border Patrol. He put on a mass flight to Alaska, and

then just as he came up with a new blast at the Navy, the Navy's *NC-4*, a huge flying boat, had the honor of first crossing the Atlantic Ocean in a series of hops. A short time later Great Britain scored in the trans-oceanic race with a nonstop flight from Newfoundland to Ireland. The British dirigible, *R-34*, crossed the Atlantic in July and returned safely. Ross and Keith Smith, two brothers, flew a Handley-Page bomber all the way from England to Australia.

All these thrilling "stunt" flights caught the attention of the public, but were headline items for but a few days. Thankful for the interest they had aroused, Mitchell rushed into print with new appeals and claims. The idea of sinking the Navy's battleships was uppermost, however, and he continued to hack away at this thought. In the summer of 1920 Mitchell organized an Army air-mapping tour of Alaska, under Captain St. Clair Streett, but although important to the Army, it did not have the universal appeal of a "stunt" flight.

Notwithstanding its success with the *NC-4* trans-Atlantic flight, the Navy played into Billy Mitchell's hands when Admiral Benson, then Chief of Naval Operations, said: "I cannot conceive of any use the U.S. Fleet will ever have for aircraft." Admiral Benson had been to Europe with an investigating board, looking into various air organizations over there. When Mitchell thought that Admiral Benson was about to issue an order abolishing the Navy's air arm, he went into his tirade again, until the Assistant Secretary of the Navy,

Franklin Delano Roosevelt, denied the report and said that the Navy had no intention of working without aviation co-operation.

General Mitchell continued to needle the Navy, however. In the summer of 1920 he was scheduled to attend the American Legion Convention in San Francisco. Everyone knew the theme he would harp on, and the Navy decided to send a smart formation of twenty-four airplanes to put on a display. Unfortunately, bad weather hit at the wrong time and the Navy aircraft were soon scattered all over California, instead of flying over San Francisco Bay to honor the Legion men. In a newspaper interview, Mitchell said, "What more can you expect from the Navy?"

He was not alone in his contempt for the battleship. Admiral Sims, who had headed America's Navy in World War I, said that the aircraft carrier would soon replace the dreadnought. Admiral Sir Percy Scott, father of British naval gunnery, was making the same claims in London. "Of what use is the battleship?" he demanded in a long letter published in the London *Times.*

This letter was still being discussed when the *London Illustrated News,* a pictorial magazine, published a sensational reply to Admiral Scott's question. In its pages two photographs showing the effects of an aerial-bomb explosion on the deck of a battleship startled the naval world. The ship's topsides, gun turrets and bridge were blown to wreckage. This battleship was none other than the U.S.S. *Indiana,* but not one of these pictures was published in an American newspaper until some weeks later.

Here is what happened. When the U. S. Navy realized that General Mitchell was putting up a very stiff argument, it decided to find out on its own just what would happen if a modern battleship were hit by an aerial bomb. Navy heads took the *Indiana,* which was about to be decommissioned, and dropped 900-pound bombs on it from navy airplanes. They hoped that the result would be so much in their favor, they would be able to put on a public display to show up Mitchell. However, Mitchell, with three other Army officers, had been invited to watch the tests, held off Hampton Roads. It was Mitchell who had obtained the photographs and some details of the bombing test, and sent them to the well-known London magazine.

The Navy was backed to the wall. General Mitchell's popularity rose to new heights, and when next he had a chance to speak before the House Appropriations Committee, he made another plea for funds with which to build up the Air Service.

"We will prove," he said again, "that money spent on naval vessels will be a criminal waste. If you will give us a collection of navy ships, we will prove that we can send them to the bottom."

Secretary of the Navy, Josephus Daniels, fought back with a statement that was to make him the laughing-stock of the military world.

"I will be glad," he bellowed, "to stand bareheaded

on the deck or at the wheel of any battleship while Mitchell takes a crack at it from the air."

It was well intentioned, but in the end the Navy was forced to agree to Mitchell's terms. It would furnish a number of obsolete naval vessels, including the former German dreadnought, *Ostfriesland* (which had fought at Jutland), and these ships would be staked out as targets. Both the Army and Navy would find out exactly what aerial bombs could do.

Chapter 9

THE AIR HAWKS GATHER

I<small>T MUST NOT</small> be presumed that Mitchell thought it would be easy to prove his Air Service could sink a naval battleship. He soon realized that he had talked himself into a very tough situation. Not that he was alone in his views. Several aviation enthusiasts in other countries spoke in his support. But to appear on lecture platforms and state in the public press that an airplane could sink a modern battleship was one thing; to prove it before a group of military experts was something else.

On his return from World War I, when it became evident that he would have to fight tooth and nail to build an Air Service worthy of the name, Billy Mitchell realized that the one way to sell the airplane to his people was to set it a task that would leave no questions unanswered. With this in mind, he decided that the world's military experts would have to be shown that battleships, without air protection, could be sunk by an airplane carrying a suitable weapon.

To provide such a spectacle was not easy. There was plenty of opposition to his plan. Navy officials were outraged at the suggestion that their Queen of the Seas, the battleship, might be found wanting. If it could be proved, it might mean the end of the Navy, which did not wish to give up rank, gold braid and positions of authority to an upstart service that flew rickety airplanes. It was hard for a Navy man to accept. All he knew, all he had been taught, was to fight the enemy on the high seas, to maneuver great surface fleets, and train batteries of big guns on seaborne targets. His viewpoint was understandable.

There were also other organizations that dreaded the prospect of an airplane sinking elements of a modern fleet. The steel business, the great shipyards and the armament factories faced extinction or bankruptcy if this wild man sank one of these expensive vessels. Big Steel, in particular, had a large stake in the American Navy. Giant dreadnoughts provided the bulk of its profit. Congress was considering the allocation of large sums of money for a large Navy, and dozens of rolling mills, foundries and docks would go out of business if the Air Service bombing plan were not forestalled.

Some men argued: "Why start a new fear in the land? These splendid surface ships are the pride of all great navies, the unchallenged guardians of the seas. They are invulnerable and indispensable, and they should remain so. This ridiculous attempt to sink one from the air, whether Mitchell succeeds or not, can only raise a great doubt in the minds of the taxpaying public. No matter what happens, Big Steel stands to lose millions of dollars."

But one small group of Navy men were in full accord with General Mitchell and secretly hoped that he would put on a convincing show. These were all young flyers of the not-so-important Naval Air Service. The few who had dared to show their interest were warned by the Navy Department to keep clear of the controversy.

In one of his rare moments of compassion, General Mitchell said, "It is psychologically impossible for a Navy man to encourage the support of an air force that is designed to destroy the very thing that a naval officer has been trained to honor and respect—the great capital ship. None of us likes to see things destroyed that we have been brought up to revere. That is human nature."

Nevertheless, Billy Mitchell continued his plans to sink one of the finest battleships ever built. His determination, public interest and the general support of the press at last provided the great opportunity. Congress agreed to submit an ex-German submarine, the *U-117;* a former German destroyer, the *G-102;* the ex-German light cruiser *Frankfurt,* weighing 5,400 tons; and the battleship *Ostfriesland* (East Frisia) which had withstood eighteen hits from the twelve- and fourteen-inch guns of the British Navy during the Battle of Jutland. She had escaped that salvo, only to run into a mine field put down by a destroyer. But the damage suffered there failed to stop her, and she staggered away through the smoke of battle and made port. Her triple hull, with eighty-five watertight compartments, and her hardened-steel armor made her 27,000 tons practically unsinkable.

The *Ostfriesland* had to be sunk. Treaty rulings demanded the destruction of this amazing vessel. The coalition of Allied powers had argued that she could not be added to the naval strength of the United States. She was offered as the sacrifice, and if Billy Mitchell's puny bombers could not sink her, the U. S. Navy battle-wagon guns would be loaded and ready to finish her. President Wilson put a deadline on the deal. The *Ostfriesland* and the other German ships were to be sunk in fifty fathoms of water by Sunday, July 24, 1921.

Once he was certain that permission would be given, Billy Mitchell began gathering his flock of air hawks to carry out the plan. There were only a few hundred trained airmen left from the 14,000 available a few years before. The call went out and every man who could fly was ordered to Langley Field, Virginia. They came from every air strip in the country, each and every one determined to do his best for General Billy. They were called The First Provisional Air Guard.

Airplanes? The best Mitchell could collect was 93. It was hopeless to include 20 old flying boats and 9 lighter-than-air blimps. A short time before, Mitchell's Western Front air force had been backed up by more than 1,500 planes. Today he had 20 *SE-5s*, 40 De Havilland bomber-reconnaissance ships, 6 Handley-Pages (the kind that General Trenchard had developed) and 6 Caproni bombers left over from the Italian Air Service.

But General Mitchell had one hope. Somewhere, on some mysterious assembly line, he had fourteen new Martin bombers, known as the Martin "Twin" because of their two 400-hp Liberty engines. There was no assurance, however, that these all-American aircraft would be ready and available.

Most of the equipment collected was obsolete. The word "crate" could have been applied to most of the machines, and no one would have made any objection. Mechanics "tinkered them up" to get them to Langley Field. On arrival they were "tinkered up" again to carry out test flights. More tinkering went on when General Mitchell ordered all planes and crews on daily bomb-dropping practice.

He gathered dozens of rafts and junk lumber, had them battened together in the general form of a battleship deck and towed out to practice areas off Hampton Roads. At the same time this First Provisional Air Brigade also "tinkered" with a bombsight that had been invented by Riley Scott, an Army man who had been experimenting with such equipment since the Wright Brothers floundered off the sand dunes at Kitty Hawk. Everything was done to "tinker" the equipment into shape.

But Billy Mitchell knew that his men were the most

important factor if he was to sink the *Ostfriesland*.
Every spare minute he had he gave to pep talks.

He told his men to take notice of the locale the Navy
had selected for these tasks, and pointed out that at
Langley Field they were only a short distance from
Hampton, one of the oldest continuously inhabited
towns in America. They were also very near to where
General McClellan's Army was equipped with the first
military aircraft ever used by American forces. (Professor Lowe's balloons scouted Yorktown in 1862.) Not
far away was the site of the British General Cornwallis's
surrender to General Washington, and nearby the
Monitor and the *Merrimac* had staged their classic
battle.

General Mitchell cited that famous encounter in
his talks: "You remember that business, boys? Ericsson,
who had invented the ironclad *Monitor,* tried to make
the Navy barnacles of his day understand that the
wooden walls of the service were obsolete. He warned
them that cannon fire would glance off the *Monitor*'s
curved iron sides, while its shot would penetrate the
oak planking of any wooden warship.

"They wouldn't listen to Ericsson either. They
laughed at *Monitor*'s iron turret, and dubbed it a pill-
box. But what the pills from that box did to the Confederate *Merrimac* is still in the history books."

Billy Mitchell stormed on, and pointed, "It all happened out there in Hampton Roads. We're going out
there and show today's admirals that we can do the
same. Now get out of here and get into the air again.

Load up with all the dummy bombs you can carry
and keep at it until you can drop one in an admiral's
lap!"

The training went on, morning and afternoon.
There was no letup. They flew through good weather
and bad, through rain and fog and that spring's eternal
thunderstorms. There was no precedent to follow. The
War in Europe had afforded little air-to-sea surface
bombing, since the enemy had had little shipping.
Mitchell's men, trained as Army flyers, had to learn
anew and face the many problems of navigation over
water, since the "enemy" targets were to be moored out
some one hundred miles off the Virginia Capes. General Mitchell was in the air with them. He flew a two-
seater, watching, begging, imploring his pilots to
sharpen up their sights and get the bombs dead on the
target. On several occasions he took his tomboy sister
Harriet with him. He had to have someone to talk or
yell to when he was putting his bombers through their
paces.

Once his men got the knack of scoring clean hits on
the tug-towed raft, Billy suddenly had a new idea. He
brought his pilots and their bombardiers together
again.

"Now listen to me. We're doing pretty well. I'm positive we can sink those light vessels, the submarine and
the destroyer, but the cruiser and the battleship may
give some trouble.

"Here's the problem. Sure, we can score direct hits
on the decks, and maybe put holes all the way through.

But it is the hulls we are after. In the big ships we have a problem and I think I have an idea. Ever hear of water shock?"

Mitchell went on to explain the principle of water shock to his men, telling them how he thought it could be of use to them in sinking the big ships. On a small scale, water shock occurs when two rocks are rapped together underwater. Anyone swimming underwater nearby when the rocks are tapped together may get an earache. This is water shock, and the rocks are water hammers.

Mitchell told his men to imagine what would happen if the earache shock were increased hundreds of times, to the magnitude of a bomb going off underwater.

"Suppose we drop a bomb alongside the hull of a cruiser or a battleship," he asked them, "what then?

". . . that's what we're going to do to the *Ostfriesland*. We'll shoot for near misses, not direct hits. A near miss will set up this water-hammer effect and pound the hull to pieces. Rivets will be punched out, plates will be bent and whole sections will have to give, letting the sea water in. We don't want direct hits. They simply make holes in the deck or blow the funnels over. We want to rip open the hull and make sure she fills up and goes down. Get it?"

They got it, and tore off a cheer that made the hangar canvas flap.

"So on all your practice runs from now on you shoot for near misses. Drop your bombs in the water along- side the big babies. In that way we'll magnify the rock-under-the-water trick a million times with TNT. We'll bust up the condenser systems. We can stop any battleship in her stride by fouling the rudder, bending the propeller shafts and springing every seam she has. We'll show 'em we can sink battleships."

As the weeks went by, the Navy contrived new problems. It wanted to run one ship without a crew and have it under radio guidance. That was fine with Billy Mitchell.

"Sure! Go ahead. That will make it much easier for us. We won't have to set our bombsights for so great a difference in our speed, as compared to a standing target. If you can get your ship up to twenty knots, that means we have a twenty-knot-easier sighting problem."

Next, the Navy decided that it would also like to be in on the aerial bombing test. It had some Martin bombers and some *F-5-Ls* available. Again General Mitchell agreed. It didn't matter to him who sank the surface ships, as long as his argument was proven.

While all the plans were being drawn, while the planes were being "tinkered" and the aircrews trained for the great experiment, Mitchell left his First Provisional Air Brigade in the hands of Major Thomas D. Malling. He then continued his campaign for Congressional funds for enlarging and strengthening his Air Service. At the same time the enemies of aviation were working just as hard to have the tests postponed or canceled altogether.

This prodded General Mitchell into new torrents of

careless speech and invective. One of the newsreel companies was showing a film taken at Langley Field, in which a stack of air bombs was scrawled with "Regards to the Navy" in chalked letters. The admirals went livid. Major General Charles T. Menoher, Chief of Military Aviation of the United States Army, sent a formal request to Secretary of War John W. Weeks, to have General Mitchell removed from office.

Secretary Weeks was shocked, but being a politician, realized that his post would be pulled out from under him if he tried to relieve Mitchell at this particular time. He held up Menoher's request for two days, and then learned of the "Regards to the Navy" newsreel. He actually made up his mind to oust General Mitchell, but after making a few quiet inquiries decided that —at this time, at least—discretion was wiser. One or two newspapers had learned of Menoher's request and Weeks's consideration to remove Mitchell, and a new battle of words resulted. Eventually the Secretary of War persuaded General Menoher to withdraw the request.

By this time General Mitchell had lost any good humor he may have had. He knew that he was dealing with men who would go to any lengths to "break" him. From that time on he became a new crusader, working hard to get his air force ready for the great test. He no longer relished public adulation or the kind words of his friends. He seldom spoke or smiled. Only his sister Harriet knew that this great strain had affected his heart.

Chapter 10

THE WORLD WATCHED
AND WAITED

T HE MORNING of June 29, 1921, was ideal for
the presentation of a military drama. It was a bright
sunny day. Seen against a background of green sea and
steel-blue sky, some fifty miles off the Cape Charles
Lightship, was a long line of Atlantic Fleet vessels. The
world, watching through the eyes of special representa-
tives and the press, must have envied those who had
front seats for this historic performance.

The *Henderson*, a naval auxiliary polished and
holystoned for the occasion, was crowded with government officials, military observers from the leading foreign powers, Cabinet members, Senators, Congress-
men and ranking officers of the Army, Navy and
Marines. Big industry was also well represented, and
tycoons vied for deck space with the socialites who

always manage to be where publicity is to be found. Top-flight columnists, military writers and special correspondents representing every news service were there, loaded down with typewriters, cameras and binoculars.

Buzzing back and forth from each of the anchored target ships was the naval-control vessel, the *Shawmut,* filled with referees and United States Navy officials. Flags and pennants whipped in the breeze, giving a distinct holiday air to the proceedings.

According to the program furnished the guests aboard the *Henderson,* the production was to be staged in five acts. First the German submarine would be attacked, then an old American battleship, the *Iowa,* was to maneuver about under radio control. The ex-German destroyer *G-102* would be next, and following her, the light cruiser *Frankfurt* would come under Billy Mitchell's rain of bombs. The chief feature of the show was the "unsinkable" *Ostfriesland.*

Aboard the *Henderson* one heard a dozen conflicting views. Many accused General Mitchell of ungentlemanly behavior and predicted that this time he would be shown up before the whole world.

"He may be able to sink the tin-sided U-boat, and he should be able to smother the destroyer with the weight of his bombs, but he'll never sink the *Ostfriesland.* That, he'll never do!"

"I wouldn't sell Billy Mitchell short. Look what he did in France."

"In France he simply bombed railroad stations, gun

emplacements and enemy troops trapped in muddy trenches. This is entirely different."

"You're right. He has real bombs out here. You'll see."

"Real bombs? It's still the same explosive. You seem to forget that he will be banging away against Krupp steel and modern naval construction."

"Listen. Those small ships will be sent quickly to the bottom with six hundred-pounders. After that Mitchell will show up with one thousand-pounders, and maybe even a few two thousand-pounders."

"Bombs weighing a ton? What will he use to fly one-ton bombs out here? You'd need a truck to haul a bomb that big."

"You watch Billy Mitchell. He'll fly them out here."

This enthusiastic aviation fan may have believed that the Air Service could do all that, but the men back at Langley Field were not so optimistic. True, Mitchell did have some large bombs available. At least he had bombs that weighed 1,000 and 2,000 pounds. What few people realized was that they had only just been assembled and shipped from the factory. The TNT explosive that had been poured into the casings would take days to cool off, so that the bombs could be detonated and made ready for the attack on the German vessels.

General Mitchell, of course, took this problem in his stride. "Pack the bombs in ice during shipment, and we'll have more ice here at Langley to stack them in until we are ready to load."

Navy officials had decided previously that nothing larger than 600-pound bombs could be used. When they learned that General Mitchell had gone to the Army Ordnance Factory and demanded a one-ton bomb that would carry 1,000 pounds of TNT they tried to stop him, but Mitchell went ahead with his plans. As a matter of fact he had argued for a two-ton missile, but settled for a one-ton weapon for the *Ostfriesland*.

On the morning of June 29 the *Henderson*'s group witnessed the beginning of the tests. Three Navy sea-planes came out of the blue, dropped a series of light bombs on the *U-117*, and in quick order sent her to the bottom. The Navy's show was well done, and the bombing, staged from 1,100 feet, was most accurate. This test was carried out so smartly that many observers had no idea what had happened. A few complained, "Well, what does that prove?"

"It proves that an airplane can drop a bomb on a warship—and sink it."

"But that was only a tin-can submarine!"

"Right. But it was a very small target, remember. If they can hit what they can see of a submarine, they sure can hit a battleship."

Billy Mitchell's chief point had already been proven, but there were still hundreds of skeptics aboard the *Henderson*.

Later that day a more spectacular show was staged. The old battleship *Iowa* had her fires started and her boilers brought up to steaming pressure, and was then sent off under radio guidance. She was to move about in an area of 25,000 square miles, and if the airmen found her they could attack with dummy bombs. Navy planes and Army blimps took part in the "search" and eventually found her. This time 25 naval aircraft attacked the target from a height of 4,000 feet. Eighty dummy bombs, some weighing 520 pounds, were dropped, but only 2 direct hits were made.

The press made the most of that pathetic effort, and discounted Mitchell's claims for air power.

The Air Service did not get a chance to show its skill until July 13. This third act was put on completely by Army airmen. Their target was *G-102,* the enemy destroyer that was drifting out at sea about a hundred miles from Langley Field. Only landtype planes were used, and the bombs were limited to 300-pounders. General Mitchell led the formation, determined to show up the Navy. The visibility was none too good, cloud banks hung low, and occasional rain squalls wiped away the intermittent patterns of sunshine.

General Billy put on an impressive performance. First he sent out a flight of old Sopwith two-seaters, types that the British had abandoned back in 1916. These creaky old-timers, under the command of Captain Baucom, went down and strafed the destroyer's deck with their machine guns. So intense was this attack, it was agreed readily that had a crew been aboard few of them could have lived topside for many minutes.

Assuming that his pursuits had "won control of the

air," Mitchell then sent in 14 De Havillands carrying 100-pound bombs. These aircraft first flew a fine formation over the *Henderson,* and before they could make their attack Mitchell sent in 16 Martin bombers loaded with 300-pounders. This force was commanded by Captain W. R. Lawson, a clever bombardier, who took the planes in at 2,000 feet. Within four minutes two direct hits had blown away a funnel and demolished the bridge. The *G-102* began to sink. Three minutes later she was hit again. Other bombers then moved in and made the most of the target. Within twenty minutes after the first bomb had struck, the ex-German destroyer went down in 100 fathoms, or 600 feet.

All well and good, but there were still many cynics aboard the *Henderson.* They argued that a destroyer, like a submarine, was a small, light shell of a vessel.

"We'll wait and see what General Mitchell can do with the *Frankfurt.* Now there's a reputable cruiser. She weighs over five thousand tons and has heavy deck and hull armor and excellent watertight compartments and bulkheads. She won't go down with a few direct hits."

The program against the *Frankfurt* called for a series of ten alternating Army and Navy attacks, divided into two phases. In the first six attacks only 250- or 300-pound bombs were to be used. This was arranged to give the Navy referees a chance to go aboard later and examine the actual damage that could be done with such missiles. As it turned out these small bombs scarcely marred the beautiful *Frankfurt*. The Navy men enjoyed sighs of relief.

"It just goes to show you. If she was under way and using her antiaircraft guns, those planes wouldn't put a bomb within half a mile of her."

Later that afternoon three Navy planes loaded with 520-pounders took up the fight. This time they dropped seven, and scored three direct hits, but three of the bombs were duds and failed to explode.

Captain Lawson took a six-ship formation in, carrying 600-pounders, but he was ordered to withdraw and await further orders. The referees wanted to go aboard again and assess the damage inflicted by the Navy bombs. As a result, Lawson and his De Havillands were kept away, circling the area until the Army captain feared he would run out of fuel.

"I have only enough gas to hang about here for fifteen minutes more," he complained.

Within ten minutes the Army men were given the white light. The bombers moved into single file and began dropping their wrath. There were several direct hits, and one 600-pounder clipped the forecastle deck and struck the water with terrific force. The explosion practically lifted the cruiser clean out of the water. She fell back, rocked and rolled for a minute, and then started to sink by the bow. It was this "water-hammer" blow that finished the *Frankfurt*. As she wallowed there in her agony, two more direct hits scored, one of which proved to be a dud. Then she began to go down.

The Navy had planned to finish the old cruiser with

heavy gunfire, but Mitchell's boys made sure that this would not be necessary. By the time the bombers, now very low on fuel, had turned for home, the *Frankfurt* nosed down, tossed her stern high, threw away her mainmast, and went to the bottom.

More than pleased, General Billy Mitchell roared back and forth in his two-seater Osprey, and watched the once lovely German cruiser sinking.

"Well, maybe he can sink destroyers and cruisers," the heartsick Navy men muttered, "but he'll never sink the *Ostfriesland*. We'll give him two days to do the job, and if she's still afloat by then—and she will be —we'll finish her with the big guns of the *Pennsylvania*. We have to sink her and that's the best way."

There were some Navy officials who were positive that it would take more than the *Pennsylvania*'s big guns. "We'll probably have to sink her with large depth charges, or even have a wrecking party go aboard to burn holes in her hull."

Bill was anxious to get at this redoubtable battle-ship. On July 20 he had every plane and pilot ready. The weather was windy, the sky overcast with low clouds, and the sea choppy. Again the whole Atlantic Fleet was on hand, and the *Henderson* accommodated some 300 notables. Many of them became seasick after the first hour at sea, but managed to recover by the time the airmen appeared overhead for their bombing runs.

Again, the Navy had compiled a set of shackling rules. Not content with making the Army men fly unnecessary distances to bomb the targets, they now demanded that as soon as a direct hit was made, the planes should withdraw and allow the referees to go aboard to assess the damage of each bomb.

The Army personnel at Langley Field, worn and weary by the weeks of intensive training, resented all these strictures. Billy Mitchell was interested only in proving that he could sink a battleship, and he rallied his men time and time again, reminding them of the importance of their efforts to the future of the Air Service.

The first formation over the old battleship was made up of Martin bombers flown by the Navy. They dropped eleven bombs and scored eleven direct hits, but their light bombs did little damage. The referees from the *Shawmut* went aboard to inspect the result, but left hurriedly when it was learned that Mitchell's planes were on the way. The Navy men had been stalling for hours, hoping someone higher up would call off the bombing tests, and get the whole affair over by having the *Pennsylvania* finish the ex-enemy target with turret gunfire.

Mitchell and his pilots, waiting for the call, were in a state of high excitement. They walked up and down the hangars, smoked incessantly, and drank innumerable cups of coffee. General Mitchell had primed them to the peak, and now the keen edge of their enthusiasm was being dulled by the inaction, the uncertainty, the old service game of "hurry up—and wait."

Actually, the Army Martins were not due over the

target until 1 P.M., but on learning of the failure of the various Navy attacks and the grim satisfaction the big Navy men were voicing over the slight damage the 230-pound bombs were inflicting, the Army pilots felt that every minute they were shackled at Langley Field deprived them of many opportunities of putting a bomb smack down a funnel on the *Ostfriesland.*

Just before lunch, unable to contain himself any longer, Billy jumped into a two-seater reconnaissance plane, and with Captain St. Clair ("Wingbone") Streett as his observer, flew out to see what was holding up the show. As they circled the Atlantic Fleet they noticed that all ships seemed to be steaming back to their offshore anchorages.

"What's going on down there?" Billy demanded.

Captain Streett, who had made radio contact, said, "They think the weather is too windy and that you won't risk flying out over the ocean. The *Henderson* is going back to Washington."

"Tell them to get back on the line. Tell them we're ready and waiting. I'll have the bombers over the target in a few minutes."

Knowing Billy Mitchell, the referees scurried off the *Ostfriesland* like rats deserting a sinking ship.

Fifty-nine minutes later, or almost exactly on the button of 1 P.M., the Army's first formation of Martin bombers appeared over the target area. Here was the opening of the final act; the grand climax. What had gone on before had been only a pip-squeak introduction. This was the display that Billy Mitchell knew must decide the future of the Air Service. If his pilots, aircraft or bombs failed now, everything he had done before would mean nothing and would soon be forgotten.

But if he succeeded—if the *Ostfriesland* went down—if his water-hammer theory was proven, all his claims for the importance of air power would be recognized publicly; accepted once and for all as military gospel. Aviation would take its place as an equal, at least, with the Army and the Navy.

The rest of the world waited and watched.

Chapter 11

THE BOMB HEARD
AROUND THE WORLD

BILLY MITCHELL's First Provisional Air Brigade went into action carrying twelve 600-pound bombs. The Navy had already dropped fifty-eight missiles that weighed 230 and 500 pounds each. Eleven antipersonnel bombs had also been released, mainly to test wind conditions and the bombsights. According to the reports from the referees, the Navy's bombs had scarcely dented the standard plates of the *Ostfriesland*'s bridge or superstructure. The gunners aboard the *Pennsylvania* were hauling a number of armor-piercing shells from the magazines below for their big guns—just in case.

The first Army formation was led by Lieutenant Clayton L. Bissell, a World War I hero who had been awarded the D.S.C. and the D.F.C. Bissell had risen to the rank of captain in that conflict, but had had to accept a reduced rank in order to stay in the service after hostilities ceased. His force, deployed in column formation and flying at an altitude of 1,500 feet, dropped five 600-pound bombs and scored two direct hits. Mitchell had asked that a number of shots be aimed for near misses, to get the "water-hammer" effect, and of course when the referees checked over the damage, the near misses were not credited.

The direct hits had set up some superficial damage, but no one mentioned that some of the hull seams below the water line had been opened up. The port engine room was flooded and the *Ostfriesland* was showing a slight list astern, but at the time none of this was mentioned by the referees. In fact a fast destroyer, the *Leary,* was hurrying a group of newspaper reporters ashore so that they could file stories explaining, ARMY FLYERS FAIL TO SINK GERMAN BATTLESHIP.

High naval officers smiled and said that the test, so far, was going exactly as they had expected. General John J. Pershing, together with Secretary of War Weeks, evidently felt much the same. They went back to Washington and decided not to return for the next day's exhibition.

Lieutenant Bissell, leading the Martin bombers, and Billy Mitchell aboard his observation plane, turned back for Virginia. On the way they ran into wicked weather, and rain squalls battered the ancient aircraft. There was considerable concern for the safety of the formation as the fuel tanks were running dry from pounding against the storm. Captain Streett, who had led Mitchell's epic flight to Alaska without losing a plane, had to plot their course by dead reckoning. They could see only a short distance in any direction, and the buffeting winds slowed the ninety-seven-mile return trip, which required one hour and forty minutes.

They finally spotted the outline of Currituck Lighthouse through the lurid, yellowish haze of the storm, and once they were flying inland the venom of the weather abated somewhat. While coursing along a narrow strip of sand that projected into Currituck Sound, Mitchell noticed one of his Martins down in a cornfield. He circled twice, until he was certain that the pilot, Lieutenant Boyd, was uninjured and that the plane had only run out of gas. Then, wondering whether the bomber could be flown out for the next day's tests, he decided to go down and look over the situation. Billy landed safely, but his plane sank into a ditch covered over with weeds.

His observer, Captain Streett, went off and rounded up a farmer and a team of horses. By dusk the aircraft was hauled out safely, and the two flyers continued on back to Langley Field.

Then began another night of plane tinkering and reloading of fuel and bombs. Number 20 Squadron had been assigned the task of carrying the 2,000-pounders that, by now, were fairly cool in their ice packs. The orders for the next day were that both the Army and the Navy were to make attacks with 1,000-pound bombs, beginning at 8 A.M. The Board of Observers also stated that as soon as one hit was made with a 1,000-pound bomb, the attack would be discontinued for ship inspection. Following the referees' report, both the Army and Navy planes would be allowed to drop three 2,000-pound bombs each. However, the Navy apparently had no access to any of Mitchell's one-tonners, and the statement meant very little.

Flying a *DH-4*, Billy Mitchell led a formation of eight Martins, each burdened with two 1,000-pound bombs. He left Captains Roberts and Stribling, two ordnance experts, to supervise the loading and adjusting of the 2,000-pounders' fuses. The Air Service had eight Martins standing by for the afternoon show with the big one-tonners. One failed to reach the target area.

Compared to the day before, July 21 was magnificent. The Atlantic Fleet was lined up two miles from the target. Near the powerful *Pennsylvania* rode the old *Olympia,* Admiral Sampson's Santiago Bay flagship; an antiquated vessel amid all the modern dreadnought strength. The monstrous, gaunt *Ostfriesland,* daubed with red lead and target markers to distinguish her from the others, sat almost motionless. There was no movement of her three stubby funnels or short, thick masts.

During the night the battleship had almost righted herself, and seemed to be riding on an even keel, although her stern appeared to be low in the water. It was learned later that water had seeped through other holes, and the old veteran had actually compensated for her distress by taking on water in opposite compartments. As a result she was still seaworthy.

General Mitchell led his first pack over the area at 8:23 A.M., circled to one side and took Lieutenant Bissell's salute as the bombers went for the target. Flying at 2,000 feet, the first plane over made a direct hit on the forecastle. With that, the officials aboard the *Shawmut* ran up a signal ordering a "Cease Fire," but the Army men were too busy making their run-ins. Four more airplanes passed over, and four more direct hits were registered.

By this time Lieutenant Bissell noted the *Shawmut*'s signal and halted the attack. When asked why he had not obeyed the order earlier, Bissell simply said, "Sir, if I was sent out to get a ship, I would get it; but if I was to obey orders, I would obey orders."

To which Mitchell added, "If we had wanted to disregard orders we could have sunk the *Ostfriesland* then and there. That was a pretty hard thing to give up at the time."

Although Mitchell's bombers still had nine 1,000-pounders left, they were ordered to return to their base, and the General followed them. In the meantime naval aircraft in the vicinity were also sent back with orders to take on fourteen-inch dummy shells filled with cement, in order to carry out armor-piercing attacks. In this way the Navy hoped to learn just what an armor-piercing shell could do against Krupp metal.

When the observers climbed aboard the target ship

this time they discovered that two of Bissell's direct hits had penetrated the *Ostfriesland*'s upper decks, but had left a protective deck intact. Considerable damage had been inflicted, but the referees decided that the battleship was still serviceable, and under war conditions would have been able to make port.

Navy officials were more confident than ever that no matter what Mitchell did now, nothing could sink the target vessel. They were so jubilant they decided that the Navy's dummy armor-piercing attack could be postponed until General Mitchell had had his opportunity to demonstrate with his 2,000-pound missiles.

A signal was sent to Langley Field and the Army bombers were told to come back and get rid of their "big boys." Practically everyone aboard the *Henderson* was positive that only the big guns of the *Pennsylvania* could bring a conclusion to this program.

General Billy Mitchell knew that this was his last chance. He no longer exhorted his pilots and crews. He probably felt that his future was in the hands of some divine Providence. Before he could send off his big bombers for the last time, he received a new order stating that his airplanes could proceed to the target, "with a maximum of only three of the giant bombs." To some extent, this overruled the previous agreement that he would be allowed to make at least two direct hits on the deck with the heaviest bombs. Billy had hoped to drop several, not worrying too much about hits on the deck, but he wanted to prove that near misses—if close enough—would be more damaging to the hull than any direct hit topside.

Mitchell signaled his "big boys" away, and sent a message to the commanding officer of the Navy's control ship: "Combined Martin and Handley-Page formation, with 2,000-pound bombs, has taken off from Langley Field. In case of failure to secure two direct hits, subsequent attacks will be made until we have secured the two hits the Army is authorized to make."

Mitchell had made the most of the Navy's tricky deal, taking advantage of the "two-direct-hits" feature of the message. There was no time to argue further, for shortly after noon the Army bombers, flying in a tight V formation and led by Captain Lawson, appeared overhead. General Mitchell was not far behind them in his two-seater Osprey.

Moving across the target at an altitude of 2,500 feet, the first "big boy" went down. Those aboard the *Henderson* gasped when they saw this monster, almost twelve feet long and eighteen inches in diameter, curve forward and head for the *Ostfriesland*. It glinted in the sunshine as it wriggled to get its nose down, and once on course, flashed like a giant dart. It chugged into a rising wave about one hundred feet off the starboard bow of the battleship. There was a muffled roar and a great geyser of water disgorged a column of black and white smoke. According to their prejudices or points of view, the observers watched with mingled opinions. Some saw it as a terrible blow; others were certain that the explosion had had no effect. To Billy Mitchell, watching from above, it was the first of his "water-hammer" blows that would eventually send the big battleship to the bottom.

The second one-tonner also "missed," and fell in the water about 300 feet ahead of the bow, but the explosion was tremendous. The bomb had detonated at the proper depth, and under the green water the black smoke of the explosive mixed with the white froth of the sea, indicating that a perfect detonation had taken place. Three thousand feet above the explosion the pilots felt a punch of concussion strong enough to tilt their planes sharply. What could that force be doing to the hull of the *Ostfriesland?* Thirty thousand tons of water had been dropped on her decks from a height of several hundred feet.

The third one-tonner smacked into the side armor a few feet aft of the bow. It glanced off and exploded in the water. This time the "hammer" lifted the big ship well out of the water, held her there, and then allowed her to flop back. There was a terrific burst of fire, and when all the smoke had filtered away a great hole could be seen in her starboard side.

Billy Mitchell was positive now that no wartime vessel would have been able to withstand all this. A ship in action would have its magazines jammed with high explosive. It would have steam condensers that would break up and scald everyone within reach. Coal bunkers or oil tanks would catch fire. But the *Ostfriesland* bore none of these pregnable features. She was simply a sitting ship with no one aboard, but with every safety device known working and holding tight.

Still, the ex-German dreadnought was afloat, and there were only four one-tonners left. The fourth one went down, spinning and fighting to gain stability. This one hit twenty-five feet off the portside amidships. The fifth lifted the great hulk clear once more. She dropped, rolled, and a Niagara of water swept over her starboard side. Two great guns ripped away from their turrets and slid into the water. With that the bow of the battleship rose as though she were crying for pity.

Someone aboard the *Henderson* said, "Pshaw, she'll float for days!"

The sixth "big boy" then slammed into the water off the starboard side. It lifted the ship's stern high and as the vessel fell back, the onlookers noticed a sharp list to port, and everyone watching knew that this was the end.

"She's sinking," they said hollowly.

Incredulous, but true. The *Ostfriesland* was sinking. Even the Army cohorts felt no particular triumph. The guests crowding the decks and bridges were stupefied. As the battleship listed sharply, her bow came up again showing another great hole. The water line on the starboard side moved up higher and higher as the list increased.

General Billy Mitchell knew that he had won. Captain Streett loosened his belt and stood up in the cockpit to cheer and wave his arms. Their airplane, dragging the General's pennant, went down and flew within 200 feet of the sinking vessel. Above them all churned a Handley-Page with one more 2,000-pounder in its rack. By 12:36 P.M., exactly eighteen minutes after the first big bomb had been dropped, the hull of the *Ostfriesland* was completely under water.

Like a congregation at a burial service, the hushed onlookers watched as the bow came up, still pleading for mercy, and then with her last great effort the hulk seemed to climb several dozen feet out of the water. She stood there, a battered monument, almost vertical. Then with a great gasp that sent out gushers of foamy wave, the *Ostfriesland* went to the bottom in 300 feet of water.

Someone muttered, "I feel I am watching the end of an era."

Like an angry eagle, Billy Mitchell nosed down with every wire and strut in his plane screaming its triumph. He roared over the surface turbulence, warm and serene in the knowledge that he had accomplished the impossible. He had hardly cleared the mortuary site when the last Handley-Page flew over and dropped the seventh one-tonner. The bomb fell dead center in the widening circles of bubbles, more a tribute to the veteran warrior than an angry blow. A military historian might have termed that bomb the *coup de grâce*, but the more knowledgeable recognized it as the triumph of the airplane over the craft that had for centuries been the chief weapon of empires.

Even though it had happened before the eyes of thousands of onlookers, few of them could believe it.

Chapter 12

THE RISING STORM

BILLY MITCHELL's triumph was complete. The result was accepted by military men the world over. Navy officials of the great powers recognized the truth of the lesson, and those who had witnessed the sinking of the *Ostfriesland* returned home and revised naval planning that had been under way since the Battle of Jutland. From this point of view, Mitchell had done the world's navies a true favor.

Although he had staged his great show mainly to prove that the Air Service deserved greater consideration, and to gain support for his ideas of an independent air force, the bombing had also set a new goal for naval aviation.

The Navy had played an unimportant but enlightening role in the tests. Its portion of the program had been planned to learn what would happen under actual war conditions. A few Navy minds, open to friendly discussion, had agreed willingly to the tests, but they wished to know more than whether an airplane could sink a capital ship.

"Let's give Mitchell the chance," they had said, "but let us learn something from it too. We want to know exactly what takes place when an armored deck is pierced. What happens if a bomb falls on a gun turret? What damage does the important bridge suffer from a direct hit, or as the result of concussion from a near miss? This knowledge is important to us."

This reasoning was sound and much might have been learned had this program been carried out solely by the Navy, instead of in co-operation with a rival force that was more intent on proving it could sink a battleship with aerial bombs.

But the few Navy airmen there were at the time made the most of Mitchell's exploit. The value of the airplane had been proven, and they argued that if this machine was of such value in the hands of the Army, there was no reason why special aircraft could not be devised and brought into the Navy's defense program. Up to now the Navy had concentrated on flying boats or float planes, on the assumption that since they were to work with oceangoing vessels, they should be equipped to land on or take off from water.

The progressive thinkers of naval aviation soon pointed out that if enemy bombers were to attack the surface fleet, the Navy would need high-speed fighters to drive them off. But these could not be built on flying-boat hulls, or haul ungainly floats. High-speed fighters capable of furnishing cover for surface craft would have to be land-type aircraft, burdened with nothing heavier than wheel gear.

"Ah yes," the critics of this idea argued, "but as soon as you rely on land planes, you will have to fly them from land bases. Let us suppose our surface navy is some 3,000 or 4,000 miles away. What fighter can you build that will have the necessary speed and maneuverability, and still have the range to go out, protect the fleet, and fly back again? How do you overcome that?"

"We'll design land-type fighters, and see what can be done about developing the aircraft carrier. The British started building carriers back in 1917. They are still experimenting and improving them. If we are going to give up building expensive battleships, why not put that money into aircraft carriers? If the British can do it, we can."

We could, and we did—thanks to General Billy Mitchell.

At that time few people realized the ultimate result of the battleship test, but today we all know that once Mitchell had proven that airplane bombs could actually sink a capital ship, the Navy had no choice but to reconsider its aviation program and develop the aircraft carrier.

It was just as well that it did, for two Japanese naval officers who had witnessed the sinking of the *Ostfriesland* hurried back to Tokyo to spread the word. Twenty years later, when Admiral Yamamoto decided to attack Pearl Harbor, the Japanese Navy had six large (fleet) and many light escort carriers. At that time the United States had only five, and it was many months before the enemy could be cut down to size. It was our flight-deck aircraft of all types that eventually enabled us to sink the Imperial Japanese Navy, exactly as Billy Mitchell had sunk the *Ostfriesland*—by air bombing.

It would be ideal, from the historian's point of view, if General Mitchell's story could be concluded with the exciting details of the bombing tests off the Virginia Capes. It would be pleasant to add that he took command of America's new Air Service and built it up to a point where it would have been efficient and ready for the outbreak of World War II; a conflict he had predicted and hoped to prepare for. We would have liked to tell the rest of the story as it should have been played out—how he rose to a four-star general, enjoyed the fruits of his effort, and gained a rewarding and honorable retirement, still the hero of the American public.

But this was not to be. Billy Mitchell was too explosive a personality to rest on his laurels. Once he had proved his point, he continued to belabor the subject at every opportunity. It must be admitted, too, that there were a number of malcontents in the Navy who refused to acknowledge the general's accomplishment. In order to convince the skeptics, Mitchell's Army bombers repeated the success in September 1923, sinking the *New Jersey* and *Virginia,* two obsolete vessels. This time the bombing was done from a height of 10,000 feet.

Now the argument went: "You said you sank the *Ostfriesland* with the 'water-hammer' blows of near misses that opened up seams in her hull. In the case of the *New Jersey* and *Virginia* your bombs failed to open hull seams, and these old battleships only went down with the weight of bombs that made direct hits on their decks."

"Well, I've proved we can sink them either way," Mitchell countered.

"Nothing of the sort. We believe that the *Ostfriesland* was a sitting duck. She had very little vertical armor about her hull, and we are not certain that all her watertight doors were in order. Who knows whether all hatches and air ports were closed?"

Mitchell laughed. "Well, you had enough people aboard before and between the bombing tests. If she wasn't battle-ready, it certainly reflects on you. I just proved that we could sink her."

The Navy men continued to argue: "The *New Jersey* and *Virginia* were not modern ships. They were quite old and had no vertical armor, either. They were mere cockleshells compared to the modern dreadnought."

"I'll tell you what I'll do," Billy Mitchell said recklessly. "Take any modern vessel you have, put her out to sea, and take all war precautions. If you'll get permission, we'll stage an attack and you can shoot at us with anything you have—and we'll still sink you!"

This boast, of course, was never accepted. In a short while Mitchell was again going up and down the country presenting his views, gaining more and more popular support, and selling the country on the value of an unified Air Service. General Menoher, who had quietly requested Mitchell's removal prior to the *Ostfriesland* display, found himself in an unenviable position, and resigned.

That same day, Billy Mitchell submitted his own resignation and requested that he be relieved of his post and assigned to other duties.

"I feel that the conditions with respect to the development of aviation, as they now exist in the War Department, make my presence in the executive organization a source of irritation, rather than a means of progressive advancement," he explained.

This occurred just eight weeks after the sinking of the German battleship, but fortunately the resignation was not accepted, and the American people knew nothing of this situation for many months.

Mitchell's popularity with the general public continued to run high, and within a short time people were clamoring for his promotion as Chief of Military Aviation. In other words, to be given the post that General Menoher had just resigned. Newspapers all over the United States printed editorials pointing out Mitchell's fitness for the post, stating that he had become a symbol of Army Aviation, and that his appointment to head the Air Service would receive instant approval.

But there was no such enthusiasm in Washington. General James G. Harbord, then Deputy Chief of Staff, advised Mitchell by note that the Secretary of

War wished him to remain at his present duties, at least until after the completion of a new set of bombing experiments scheduled for late in September. To that General Harbord also added, "If after the conclusion of these exercises, Mitchell should still desire to retire from office, he may submit his resignation again."

In the meantime, Secretary Weeks called in General Mason M. Patrick, who had served as Chief of the Air Service in France, and offered him General Menoher's post.

Whether Mitchell knew of this is not certain, but at any rate he busied himself with the new exercise, one in which the old and partly dismantled battleship *Alabama* was to be used as a target. In this test a varied program of gas and smoke bombs, smoke screens and night-attack problems were to be worked out. In one feature of the test, mines and torpedoes were to be launched, but according to Mitchell, none were available. The Navy refused to provide them unless a very high price was paid for each weapon.

The *Alabama* test, set up for three days, was something of an anticlimax after the *Ostfriesland* spectacle, but the public and newspapers seemed to show unusual interest. Every type of available bomb was used, and the referees discovered what great fires, poison gas and smoke screens these chemicals and explosives could create. But again, it was Mitchell's 2,000-pound bombs that finally sent the old battleship to the bottom.

Once this affair was out of the way, Mitchell returned to Washington where he learned that General

Patrick had been installed as Chief of the Air Service. The two men had got on well together during the First World War, and to the surprise of many, Billy Mitchell accepted the situation in good spirit. He planned to present all his latest ideas to his new chief in the belief that General Patrick would accept them in friendly co-operation.

In October, Patrick, a nonflying administrator, called in Mitchell for a special conference. Whatever happened at that meeting in no way eased the situation. General Patrick let it be known that he was willing to listen to Mitchell's suggestions, but stated clearly that he intended to act as Air Chief in actions, as well as in name. All final decisions would be made by him.

Mitchell, who by now was having some trouble with his heart and showed certain symptoms of physical weariness, was in no mood to accept General Patrick's attitude.

"I'm sorry, sir," he said, "but I cannot continue to serve under these conditions. I have decided to tender my resignation."

"In that case, General," Patrick is said to have replied, "let us go in to see General Harbord, where you can submit your resignation formally."

That was on Saturday afternoon, October 14, and General Harbord had left for the weekend. Over the next few days Mitchell apparently cooled down and reconsidered, for when Patrick again escorted him in to see Harbord, Billy said wearily, "I have thought the matter over, and have decided not to resign. Instead,

I will assist General Patrick along the lines which he has laid down."

Because of their past friendship, General Patrick wrote a definite set of arrangements defining Mitchell's powers, and they parted the best of friends. Secretary of War Weeks used this situation to warn Mitchell that in the future if he planned to make any public announcements, or write articles for military magazines, he would have to submit his statements to the War Department for approval. To keep him reasonably quiet, Secretary Weeks sent Mitchell to Europe at the head of a mission to study the progress of aviation there. France, Great Britain, Germany, Holland and Italy were visited and the American group picked up many new trends in military aviation. Mitchell also used the trip to gather ammunition for his next blasts at the aviation situation at home. For one thing, he discovered that the military spirit in Germany was far from being crushed. His Teutonic hosts complained continually of the limitations imposed on their aircraft industry by the Versailles Treaty.

"I noticed, however," he commented, "that they still manage to design and build practical aircraft that are second to none anywhere. The Versailles Treaty doesn't seem to have hampered them to any great extent."

On his return to the United States, Billy continued his campaign to build up the Air Service. He became something of a flying inspector-general, roaring from one field to another. He worked his men at top speed, and encouraged everyone to make the most of what he had, and to keep the standards of flying high. Despite his heart condition, Billy continued to be involved in hair-raising flights and dangerous stunts in order to prove that he was the service's flying general. He took part in air races and staged impromptu acrobatics around Washington's monuments, giving most of his superiors fits of breathless terror. In an air meet held at Detroit on October 18, 1922, he established a new speed record of 224.38 miles an hour in an Army Curtiss airplane. He was almost forty-three years of age at the time, but he had brought the world's aviation mark to America, and added to his stature as a leader of men.

All this promotion on his part eventually resulted in the Lassiter Board's recommendation of the adoption of a ten-year aviation plan that would have allotted $25,000,000 a year to establish a peacetime Air Service of 4,000 officers, 2,500 flying cadets, 25,000 enlisted men and 2,500 airplanes. Mitchell's plea for a unified Air Service went unheeded. Secretary Weeks approved the Lassiter recommendations, but they were sidetracked and sent to a joint Army-Navy Board where they remained in some dusty pigeonhole. Thirty months went by and still the old wartime American-built De Havillands were living up to their reputations as "Flying Coffins." Crashes and tragedies were reported regularly, and air crews were wiped out almost every week.

Captain Lawson, the man who had led the Martin bombers in the successful attack on the *Ostfriesland,* was lost with his crew in one of these obsolete aircraft. His death sent Billy Mitchell off on another of his crusading rampages. This was shortly after America had sworn in a new President, Calvin Coolidge, who started his administration with an economy drive. Military aviation, to him nothing more than an outlet for young officers flying around the country burning up government gasoline, was the first to come under his critical eye.

Nevertheless, Mitchell continued to point out that big expenditures for naval equipment would be better spent on building up the Air Service. Then came the test in which Army bombers sank the battleships *New Jersey* and *Virginia,* vessels that had been rated as obsolete through the new Naval Limitations Treaty. Despite this further success, General Pershing, who had never actually accepted the airplane as a military weapon, announced that these latest tests only proved the accuracy of the bomber's aim, but did not prove that warships could be sunk under wartime conditions. And so the effect of the bombing against the old battleships was ignored.

Wisely, General Patrick sent Billy Mitchell to Hawaii to make a survey of the military situation in the Pacific. He was away for nine months, and after a very diligent investigation, returned to report that American defenses out there were far from adequate and lacked full co-ordination between the Army and the Navy.

General C. P. Summerall, in command of the Hawaiian area, took violent exception to Mitchell's report, and said that it had been written only to expound the cause of air power. To a certain extent General Patrick agreed with General Summerall, but did his best to smooth over the situation.

It was the same wherever Mitchell went in the far Pacific. In the Philippines he predicted what would happen if an enemy decided to challenge America's right in the Far East. In the Dutch East Indies, Siam, India and elsewhere he applied his belief in air power to the obvious military situation. None of it pleased him . . . and he said so.

Billy Mitchell realized his country's inadequacy, if ever a war should develop. More important, he returned from Japan with vital information on the growing Japanese air power.

But it was useless to expound on these points. The Lassiter recommendation was still being shuffled from department to department. The country had apparently retired into its old isolationist shell, and military matters were of no importance. During this Jazz Age era, political corruption, widespread bootlegging of illegal liquor and a tragic-comic provincialism held the stage.

American airmen had won thirty-three of the forty-two flying records, but as the French Undersecretary for Air expressed it: "You have the records, yes; but they are only the façade. Behind them is nothing. You cannot fight a war with records. You must have planes. Lots of planes."

Unable to halt the rising tide of Mitchell's popularity and influence, Secretary of War Weeks still held a secret weapon. When Billy was made a brigadier general in 1918, it was only a temporary commission. Under normal routine his rank would have reverted to that of a colonel after the War, but since he had been appointed for a term as Assistant Chief of Air Service in the United States, he was permitted to retain his wartime rank. When that term was up he would become a colonel—unless he was reappointed.

This term was up in April 1925, and the President would reappoint him only if the Secretary of War made the recommendation. As may be imagined, taunted by Mitchell's continued firebrand behavior, Secretary Weeks refused.

The military ax fell. Shortly after, Colonel William Mitchell was deprived of his Assistant-Chief-of-Air-Service post, and was "exiled" to San Antonio, Texas, where he was given the duties of Air Officer, Eighth Corps, at Fort Sam Houston.

Within six months Billy Mitchell had unleashed a new storm on the issue of air power that eventually brought about his court-martial and a series of penalties that hastened his death.

Chapter 13

THE FINAL STRAW

The U. S. Navy dirigible Shenandoah, under Commanders Zachary Lansdowne and Charles Rosendahl, left its mooring mast at Lakehurst, New Jersey, on September 2, 1925, and headed west on a "goodwill" cruise as far as Minneapolis, showing the airship over State fairs on the way.

On September 1, Commander John Rodgers, a descendant of the famous naval family, was missing somewhere in the Pacific. Commander Rodgers had been attempting to fly a naval seaplane nonstop from San Francisco to Hawaii. His last message indicated that although he was somewhere within 300 miles of his goal, he was running short of gasoline. This was the last that was heard of Commander Rodgers and his crew of four for about ten days.

The Navy admitted that Rodgers's plane carried only enough fuel to make the trip—if aided by favorable winds. It was explained that on August 31 the winds were favorable, but had reversed when the Navy flying boat started out the next day.

The "exiled" Billy Mitchell went on the radio at San Antonio and said, "I ask my listeners to pray for the American airmen down in the Pacific. They are just as much martyrs to the progress of civilization as Columbus would have been had he perished on his voyage to America."

But, fortunately, this first attempt at a nonstop flight across the Pacific ended on a note of triumph. Commander Rodgers and his crew rigged a sail and brought their seaplane into the island of Jaui. More important, they had made a record nonstop flight of 1,992 miles before they were forced down.

In the meantime the Shenandoah ran into tragedy. On reaching the Ohio River on September 3, the airship sailed into a severe electrical storm and a vicious line squall that broke the dirigible into two sections. One, with Commander Lansdowne and thirteen members of the crew, fell out of control and crashed, killing all fourteen men. A smaller section, with Lieutenant Commander Rosendahl in it, was handled as a free balloon and brought safely to earth.

Mrs. Lansdowne, the widow of the airship's commander, charged that her husband had protested against making the cruise because of the anticipated storm, but that he had been ordered to proceed on the journey for political reasons.

Realizing that Billy Mitchell could provide them

with a sensational comment, newspaper editors begged for his views. At first Mitchell refused, saying that he did not know the full details of the two flights. He added that he might have something for them later that day. He knew that Commander Rodgers's flight to Hawaii had been planned as an answer to his continued slurs on the Navy, and that the Shenandoah's cruise had been set up to prove that the Navy was still the first line of defense, whether it employed battleships on the sea or aircraft in the sky.

Within forty-eight hours after the Shenandoah had broken in two and crashed, Mitchell put out his most severe blast. It was a lengthy statement and was given to the Associated Press, which meant that it would appear in practically every home-town paper that night.

His critical comments included every statement he had made before, intensified and delivered with more accusation. He charged bluntly that the two accidents were the direct results of incompetency, criminal negligence and almost treasonable administration of the national defense by the War and Navy Departments. He contended that the conduct of aviation by these two departments had been "so disgusting in the last few years as to make any self-respecting person ashamed of the cloth he wears." He also said:

"All aviation policies, schemes and systems are dictated by the nonflying officers of the Army and Navy, who know practically nothing about it. The lives of the airmen are being used merely as pawns in their hands.

"The great Congress of the United States, that makes laws for the organization and use of our air, land and water forces is treated by these two departments as if it were an organization created for their benefit. Officers and agents sent by the War and Navy Departments to Congress have almost always given incomplete, misleading or false information about aeronautics; either intentionally or as the result of such gross ignorance of the question that they should not be allowed to appear before a legislative body."

Billy Mitchell described the Hawaiian flight as a "publicity stunt," and said that if the plane had carried only two men and more fuel it could have made the hop. He said that the Shenandoah flight was nothing more than "a propaganda mission"; that Fleet maneuvers held that spring in the Pacific had been "nothing more than a naval parade," and that the failure of the MacMillan Arctic Expedition was due to Navy sponsorship and the use of the wrong type of aircraft.

No officer in all history had ever gone to such lengths to criticize the command of the national defense. Mitchell knew what the blast would mean, and he accepted the fact that he would have to resign and, in all probability, face a court-martial.

Washington was stunned. Secretary of the Navy Wilbur was speechless. There was mild consternation at President Coolidge's summer White House at Swampscott, Massachusetts.

Everyone knew that this was the finish for the ex-general, but by the same token it was realized that before he went out Billy Mitchell would furnish a display of fireworks that would leave the mossback officials dazed.

At this time Billy Mitchell was not a wealthy man; the family fortunes had not kept pace with the heavy expenditures of the whole Mitchell clan. He was not poor, but he knew that if he were removed from his Army post, he would have to return to his gentleman's farming business; or his lectures and writing advocating service unification would have to pay his expenses.

Commander Rodgers and his crew suddenly turned up safe nine days after their disappearance, and Admiral Moffett, Chief of Naval Aviation, took this opportunity to denounce Mitchell as a man "of unsound mind, suffering from delusions of grandeur." He warned the country against military officers making a political appeal over the heads of Congress, direct to the people, and suggested that any such move might be the opening wedge for military dictatorship in the United States.

Billy Mitchell wisely ignored the inference.

Then President Coolidge appointed an impartial board of nine well-known citizens, under Dwight D. Morrow, to make a study of the best means of developing and applying aircraft to the national defense. This was known as the Morrow Board. At the same time Navy Secretary Wilbur appointed a naval court of inquiry to look into the Shenandoah disaster. While these boards were being selected the country sat back and awaited the arrest and court-martial of Colonel Mitchell who had been ordered to Washington to stand by as a witness for the Morrow Board inquiry.

The newspapers assumed that Mitchell had been relieved of all duty, and much was made of the fact that he had been brought to the Capital. He was met by great crowds, the full force of the American Legion and a drum-and-fife band. The next day Billy was the guest of the "Forty and Eight," an exclusive chapter of the Legion; was driven down Pennsylvania Avenue in a horse-drawn victoria, and feted at a mass barbecue. No matter where he went great crowds gathered and there were wild scenes of enthusiasm. When he appeared before the Morrow Board, Mitchell made the most of his opportunity and read a 30,000-word statement in favor of a large and independent Air Service, in which he made all his old charges against bureaucracy and Navy blundering. No one was spared. He argued that Alaska was our key defense position in the Pacific, and that one day Japan would strike through Alaska and probably drive American forces back behind the Rocky Mountains. This tirade went on for two long days.

Commander Rodgers was hurried back from the Pacific adventure to testify, and although he resented Mitchell's criticism of the ill-fated Pacific hop, he agreed that there was something vitally wrong with the Navy Department, and urged its immediate reorganization. He was in full accord with Mitchell's view of unified command, and said that he had hoped for the same thing in Naval Aviation.

While the Morrow Board investigation was in progress, the inquiry into the Shenandoah disaster added to the fuel of the Mitchell fire. Witness after witness nailed down the fact that the airship never should have been sent out on that flight at that particular time of the month. Mitchell's claim that the flight was nothing more than an unwarranted propaganda mission appeared to be justified. With that, the newspapers went after Secretary of the Navy Wilbur, and demanded his resignation. When Colonel Mitchell was called before the Navy Board to account for his criticism of the Shenandoah disaster, he made the most of this opportunity to turn the investigation into another platform from which to deliver his lecture on the importance of air power.

A popular weekly of the time, *Liberty* magazine, awarded Colonel Mitchell its regular prize of $1,000 "for distinguished moral courage," and the colonel immediately turned over the check to Mrs. Zachary Lansdowne for the dependents of the enlisted men who had died in the Shenandoah accident.

When the American Legion opened its national convention that year, President Coolidge felt compelled to appear and state that, "Any organization of men in the military service bent on inflaming the public mind for the purpose of forcing government action through the pressure of public opinion, is in an exceedingly dangerous undertaking." But the convention ignored the warning and passed a resolution favoring a unified Air Service.

Shortly after the closing of the Morrow Board hearings, Secretary of War Weeks resigned because of illness. His post was taken by Dwight F. Davis, whose first task was to announce the long-awaited court-martial of Colonel William Mitchell; scheduled to begin October 28. Secretary Davis announced that Colonel Mitchell would be tried under Article 96, known in the service as the "Old Mother Hubbard," for it was considered the most all-inclusive article in the book. In general it accused him of actions and behavior unbecoming an officer, and could be applied to any one of dozens of everyday situations. It will be noted that Colonel Mitchell was not charged with any specific crime; simply that he had behaved in a manner unbecoming an officer.

Although Billy Mitchell had been relieved of his duties in Texas and brought up on charges to face a military court-martial, there was nothing in his history on which any panel of judges could base a conviction. No sooner had the court convened than it was obvious that the military prosecutor had very little to stand on. On the other hand, the defense was able to produce witness after witness to attest to Mitchell's statements that the Air Service was being sadly mismanaged, neglected and ignored in the program of national defense.

Whether Billy Mitchell had gone about his campaign in a dignified manner was not part of the charges. True, he had been loud and boisterous, and used every publicity means available to achieve his end. But no one could argue that he was unpatriotic, treasonable or lacking in a true love for his country.

We have seen that from his early life he had been bold, forward and flamboyant, and had known that his clever use of words could sway people. But there were many other men in high government and military positions who believed just as firmly in their own opinions on what national defense required. None of them lacked patriotism or sincere love for their country. In this case America had the high-spirited military man who, by his service traditions, should have worked through routine channels to make his opinions and ideas known. But he realized that he was shackled in his conflict with freewheeling politicians who had no service traditions of behavior, "as an officer and a gentleman," to live up to.

It was on this point that the court finally found him guilty—his pattern of behavior as an officer, the violation of the 96th Article of War, and acting in defiance toward his military superiors. Billy Mitchell was suspended from rank, command and duty, with forfeiture of all pay and allowances for five years.

In other words ex-General William E. Mitchell was now Private Mitchell, a man with no authority, pay or allowances. Two days after the sentence, President Coolidge confirmed the finding. Colonel Mitchell had no choice but to tender his resignation from the Army. It was to take effect on February 1, 1926.

Billy Mitchell had been foolhardy, and had undermined service discipline for many months. Had the charge of incompetency been made and established, he should have been discharged from the service at once. The best he could be convicted of was insubordination. This left the decision open to endless debate, for under certain circumstances Billy Mitchell's faults could have been valuable military virtues.

He had argued for a unified air force on an equal footing with the Army and Navy. World War II proved most of Billy's thunderous claims. We established such a force, which in itself is an official admission that he was right, and that no matter what the outcome of the court-martial, he was fully cleared and justified. His only mistake was that he had argued too vehemently.

Civilians have little concern for Army Regulations or the Articles of War, and vehemence is no crime until it reaches some stage of disorderly conduct. But Billy Mitchell was not tried by civilians. His judges were military men who viewed his behavior as an infraction of service discipline, which is a very serious *military* crime. On such a charge he was technically guilty. But no military court-martial would sentence a man to a dishonorable discharge for any technical infraction of discipline. Billy Mitchell was not dismissed from the service—he was suspended for five years with loss of rank and pay. He had no other course but to resign and withdraw to civilian life.

Since then public opinion has argued that there should be a better means of maintaining discipline than depriving the service of one of its most able and brilliant officers at the moment when he has reached the height of his intellectual powers, with promise of many more years of valuable service.

Billy Mitchell was a patriotic American. His whole life was dedicated to the service of his country—as a soldier, not as a politician. With his background he could have completed his university education, enjoyed the benefits of foreign travel, and lived the life of a son of a wealthy man. His future, whether he took up banking or agriculture and cattle breeding, was assured. Had he been a "practical" man instead of a patriot, there is no knowing how high in his country's social scale he might have risen. Instead, he chose to become a soldier, eventually earned the pay of a temporary brigadier general, and because of his patriotism . . . wound up a private.

His personal experiences in Cuba, the Philippines, Alaska, France and other military posts had taught him many things about the importance of national defense. His was practical knowledge, not theory. In aviation, in particular, his thinking was years ahead of anyone else's in his own country. He had flown combat patrols on a war front and knew the values and limitations of the airplane. His depth of thinking told him that air power, as a unified force, would be necessary if a global conflict ever again enveloped civilization. He was positive he was right, and did all in his power to prove it to his countrymen.

In 1925, after Mitchell had shown on several occasions that the airplane could sink any type of surface vessel—whether a sliver of metal known as a submarine, or the dreadnought of all navies, the battleship—few officials listened to his warnings. Instead, politicians were ruthlessly slashing the total appropriation for national defense. Every dollar spent on aviation had to be begged from funds allotted the Army for new cavalry saddles, stainless-steel sabres and fancy booklets on open-order military tactics. Although the airplane had had an important part in World War I, few groundlings in the infantry, cavalry or artillery showed the slightest interest in the machine. As a matter of fact, most of them had forgotten that something called a tank had been invented to break up trench warfare.

By that year American military aviation was almost extinct, and Billy Mitchell was a lone voice pleading for its survival. He was certain that these dilatory measures were inviting defeat and ruin. He believed that the one way to national security was to put the Air Service under the command of experienced flying men, responsible to no authority except that of a civilian Secretary for Air under the President.

At no time did he argue for the release of aviation from top-civilian control. He had long accepted the rule that all armed men in uniform at the highest level must be answerable to unarmed civilians. It was from the General Staff down, not up, that he demanded a unified force. But his superiors were not flying men, and one and all found it difficult to give up the old traditional dogma, so prized in army posts from one end of the country to the other.

Whether we accuse Mitchell's opponents of prehistoric thinking is not of great importance. The fact is, this was how they thought, and most believed that they were right. Since they were responsible for military policy, they acted accordingly.

Mitchell knew that if he hoped to carry his message and demands further to rescue American aviation from the pit of obsolescence, he would have to use methods that would leave him open to court-martial charges. If he kept his peace, bowing to the rule that "silence gives consent," he would be consenting to a policy he *knew* to be dangerous and possibly ruinous. He probably felt that silence in this case was skirting very close to his interpretation of treason.

His must have been a difficult decision. People are prone to think him headstrong in his final moves and statements, but his eventual decision came after many months of deliberation and after long talks with true friends, both in and out of the military services. It was no last-minute flare-up, or thoughtless challenge. Actually, he took the lesser of two evils. He had either to risk being accused publicly as a loud-mouthed, un-disciplined, publicity-seeking soldier, or be forever branded by his own conscience as a man who had failed to discharge his duty to his country. He had, in the final analysis, chosen a public, in preference to a private, disgrace.

Thus, his career as a soldier-airman does not end in tragedy or unrelieved gloom, but in a mellow glow of great accomplishment. In the end—civilian or soldier—he remained one of his country's great defenders.

Chapter 14

A FIGHTER TO THE END

Discarded and renounced, Billy Mitchell retired to a small estate he called "Boxwood." It nestled in the Piedmont Valley of Virginia, about forty miles west of Washington. Nearby was the village of Middleburg, in the heart of the Bull Run Mountains. This is true riding country, and the sportsmen of Middleburg, Aldie, Boyce and Leesburg were more interested in horses than in politics or the problems of government. Across the beautiful fields, along the wooded trails and around the measured tracks, they bred, trained and schooled some of the finest mounts in America. It was good country with a pleasant climate.

Once he had freed himself of the shackles of unsympathetic authority and the frenzy and turmoil of Washington, life there should have been a great relief to Billy Mitchell. Mrs. Mitchell hoped it would turn out that way; that the horses, dogs and wildlife of the area would afford new interests—and perhaps some modest income—and that the easygoing life by woods and streams would encourage her husband to slow down and enjoy a well-earned leisure. The house was filled with books, and the gun-room racks held two hundred rifles and shotguns, dozens of fine bamboo and steel rods and tackle cases that abounded with lures and reels from all over the world.

Mitchell had reached his forty-sixth year, and considering everything, had earned a few months of real rest. His closest friends and relatives knew that he had suffered several heart disturbances. These were not serious at the time, and had he listened to his physicians and taken a full year off he might have recovered fully. If he could have ignored all the frustrations and setbacks that had concluded his service, he might have been restored to good health. But the newspapers would not let his case rest. They continued to rehash his court-martial. They knew that Mitchell was always available for a good story. They taunted him with the inference that he had withdrawn to Virginia to become a gentleman farmer and had accepted his defeat by the Top Brass of the Army.

That was all that Mitchell needed. Within a short time Boxwood's recreation, trout streams and hunting cover no longer appealed. From 1926 to 1936 this sylvan retreat was only the headquarters for his new crusade. He began a coast-to-coast lecture tour with undiminished zeal, a chore that would have put any ordinary man in the hospital. Magazines and newspapers begged for and obtained article after article, each one as sensational as anything he had written before.

Sweeping charges appeared in the *Saturday Evening Post, Review of Reviews, Liberty* and the *National Geographic Magazine.* The leading aviation magazines of the day, *Aero Digest, Aircraft Journal, U.S. Air Services* and *Aeronautics* appeared regularly with one of Mitchell's latest pronouncements. The British aero journals, *Flight* and *Aeroplane,* ran a Mitchell article every time they could, for his crusade was appreciated as much by the Royal Air Force as by the U. S. Aviation Service. Important newspapers from coast to coast seldom went to press without a Mitchell feature or at least a letter signed by him; items which prodded and jabbed at the politicians and bureaucrats who had driven him out of the Army.

After each long trail of the lecture circuit, Billy would crawl back to Boxwood, weary, bonetired and mentally exhausted. His wife did her best to keep him at home, knowing that he was driving himself to the brink. He would rest for a few days, find peace and quiet in the woods, and then on returning to his fireside, he would pick up another newspaper that carried a new taunt. Letters flowed in from aviation enthusiasts all over the country, and new subjects would race through his mind. High-school boys begged for information to help them with their term papers, or for material with which to stage a debate on the future of air power.

The Mitchells never ignored a letter. Every request was answered, and hundreds of new subjects resulted from these queries. Cranks and amateur inventors submitted their ideas for newer and faster fighters, larger bombers, freak weapons, bombs that would end all wars and fuels that would fly a formation of warplanes around the world nonstop. Billy appreciated their interest and gladly answered every note or inquiry.

The minute the letter pile went down, he was off again, mounting the lecture platforms in cities, villages, colleges, State Capitals and sometimes in churches. He never gave up presenting his views to any group that would collect to hear him.

Mrs. Mitchell, a superb horsewoman, did her best to keep the stock farm going. She exercised the mounts, schooled the show horses, and supervised the planting and harvesting of the crops. She played a very important role in his last years, for at Boxwood there was always something comforting to return to when Billy came back from what he called his "barnstorming tours." His first child Lucy grew up amid all this joyous activity. The house was more than a hundred years old, built of fieldstone, and with many unusual rooms. Some were large enough to stage a Christmas ball. On the hearthstone of one fireplace was the imprint of a dinosaur's foot. There were friendly ghosts in some of the rooms for the little girl to chase, but according to the legends only the Mitchell dogs ever actually saw them.

Little Lucy soon learned to ride and fish for trout. When her father was away she would spend hours in his studio, making up tales about the animals whose heads were mounted on the walls. She pored through his war books, and studied the hundreds of photographs he had taken all over the world. Later on, after Billy Jr. arrived, she assumed command and told all these wonderful stories again.

Whenever their father returned home from one of his trips he gave them hours of his time, thrilling or amusing them with new stories, or rehashing his old adventures. This was better than any regular classroom, for he could teach geography first hand. He had been everywhere, and when he took a globe and ran his fingers from city to city and country to country it was never a dry-as-dust lesson. It was always a great thrill and a new way to learn of the outside world. Their father told them that in their lifetime nothing would be inaccessible—space would dissolve and time would require new meanings.

Billy Mitchell was not an arrogant rebel to his children. All they ever saw was a buoyant companion, a devoted storyteller, a patient teacher and a kind man who understood their every whim and desire. Had anyone told them in those early days that their father had been up on charges before an Army court-martial, and had been found guilty of "behavior unbecoming an

officer and a gentleman," they would have been breathless with astonishment.

Meanwhile the world outside cringed under the first
tremors of a new conflict. Japan, haughty and proud
with a great army and the third most important navy
in the world, defied the tottering League of Nations
and ransacked Manchuria. Billy Mitchell recognized
the symptoms immediately and said, "The Japanese
are putting it over on an incompetent European world,
and this includes ourselves. Take my word for it, some
day we will have an armed conflict with them."

He continued these digs at the people of the Rising
Sun, and the pacifist newspapers quickly turned on
him, claiming he was a warmonger and rattling the
rifle bolt. But Mitchell kept on writing and talking. He
wrote in 1932, with the pages of *Liberty* wide open to
him, "Will Japan try to conquer the United States?"
and in another article he asked, "Are we ready for war
with Japan? These people are working almost with
desperation to make themselves the strongest military
nation in the world. Their principal aim in doing this
is in order to fight the one great white nation on the
Pacific Ocean. The United States."

He also pointed out that when he was last in Hawaii
the U. S. Army commander there would not speak to
the U. S. officer commanding the Navy, and that what
planning was done was carried out separately—a foolish
and dangerous practice.

With his teeth well into Japan, Mitchell produced

other articles in which he declared that one day the Japanese would use surprise tactics, would not go through the formality of declaring war, and would attack Alaska immediately and concentrate on Dutch Harbor in the Aleutians. He was not far wrong, for eventually—after Pearl Harbor—the Aleutians were stormed and held for a short time.

His warnings were sound and reliable, but no official attention was paid to them. After all, the Pacific Ocean was the Navy's responsibility, and whatever defense was put up would be provided by surface ships, not aircraft. In a few instances it might be possible for some aircraft to *assist* the Navy.

That same year, owing to Mitchell's continued harping for a unified service, the U. S. Air Service was transformed into the Army Air Corps and given a few opportunities to operate on its own. More important, a new office had been created in the War Department, to be headed by an Assistant Secretary of Air.

With the election of a new Democratic President, and the overthrow of the Republicans who had given Billy Mitchell so much trouble for such a long time, it was hoped that Mitchell would be given this new aviation post.

Mitchell himself had high hopes and planned to get to President Roosevelt and present his plans for the reorganization of the Army's aviation forces. He received letters from hundreds of friends, all begging him to make some definite effort to gain this position, "to take our Air Corps and Civil Aviation that our broken bodies have made possible, out of the hands of the politicians."

Shortly after the Roosevelts moved into the White House, Mr. and Mrs. William E. Mitchell were invited to lunch. There were several confidential interviews between Billy Mitchell and the new President, and the newspapers predicted that the Secretary of Air post would be Mitchell's. Several influential members of Congress and other advisers to the President warmly recommended the appointment.

The appointment was never made, and Mitchell returned to Boxwood completely crestfallen.

No explanation was ever offered, but it will be remembered that the new President had once been the Assistant Secretary of the Navy and probably had no particular fondness for Mitchell. He had seen what Mitchell's bombers had done to the Navy's battleships, and for some reason could never again warm up to the deposed Air Service officer.

After that Mitchell seemed to lose some of the force that had made his name known around the world. He continued his crusade, but his zest was gone. He wrote a few more articles and then decided to concentrate on books. He felt that solid volumes in hard covers, published by reputable editors, would have more lasting power than magazine articles that were usually skimmed over and then thrown away and forgotten.

He wrote five books in the next three or four years, only two of which were published. He spent a great deal of time rewriting his Alaskan adventures, but they were never printed. He then decided to retell his story of World War I, but the editors of that day presumed that America was tired of war and the talk of war. That volume also failed to get into print. According to those who have looked over the typescripts, his books had very little literary value. Perhaps much of the effort was blunted by his continued campaign for aviation reform and a unified service.

But Germany and Japan were both devoting every hour and every effort to building up their armed forces —particularly their air services. Since, like Great Britain, Japan was an island empire, her chief interest lay on the sea, and it was Billy Mitchell who first disclosed that Nippon was building an unusual number of aircraft carriers, and developing aircraft to operate from them.

He pointed out that Germany was building up a great army, backed up by strong tank forces, and an air service that had no equal anywhere in Europe.

Billy Mitchell was aware of all these things, and tried manfully to warn his country of the obvious danger.

His warnings went unheeded.

However, in Germany and Japan important military magazines reprinted every article Mitchell had written. His views and theories were studied carefully in Berlin and Tokyo. Although recognition was denied him in his own country, our future enemies were paying him a great compliment by teaching his lessons in their own military classrooms.

Billy Mitchell made his last important public ap-

pearance on February 11, 1935, when he addressed the
House Military Affairs Committee and once more presented his theory of our defense in the Pacific.

"Alaska is the most central place in the world," he
began, "and this is true either of Europe, Asia or North
America. I believe whoever holds Alaska will command the world." He was repeating his argument that
the northern top of our globe offers the shortest distances for striking at any adversaries of the United
States. Again, he was taking issue with the Navy's
point of view which held that the Panama Canal was
America's most important single element of defense.
He wrung his hands over the fact that by purchasing
the Virgin Islands from Denmark, "we had relin-
quished all our rights of discovery and proprietorship
to Grantland, which lies in the Arctic Ocean, abreast of
the northern tip of Greenland." To Billy Mitchell,
Grantland was one of the most important areas in the
world for an air base because it is almost equidistant
from the centers of population in Europe, Asia and
America.

Strangely enough, although earlier he had predicted
that the German nation would rise from its 1914-18 defeat and strike again, Mitchell failed to notice the real
threat of Adolf Hitler. Apparently the threat of
Nazism did not catch his imagination. Instead, he continued to fret over the possibility of Japanese aggression
in the Pacific. What few articles he now wrote for the
press all dwelt on the threat from Japan.

"It is not with Europe that our greatest future con-

cern lies," he stated again and again. "It is the Far
East. We may consider that white civilization has passed
through several periods. There was the Mediterranean
period, from which the Romans emerged victorious,
followed by the Atlantic period, which the last war
(World War I) probably ended. The United States
emerged from it as the most powerful country. Now we
are entering on a Pacific period. Straight across on the
other side of this great ocean is the Empire of Japan,
reaching out for world domination. Any idea that the
Japanese are not doing so is entirely without foundation. They are not only organizing to dominate the
whole of Asia, but to extend this domination to the
whole world. The only thing that will deter them is
armed force. Whenever the Japanese see a weak military power near them, they pounce on it if they have
anything to gain. The Japanese consider us a decadent
military power. They consider that on account of the
riches we possess, the easy existence we have led, and
the false theories that have grown up among us as to
national defense, that in a little while we shall be as
easy to attack as a large jellyfish."

Little notice was taken of his views by the men who
were responsible for the military defense of the country. America was too busy clawing its way back from a
long-drawn-out financial depression. There was no time
for the statements of a fanatic military man who had
been relieved of his commission and driven out of the
Army. Only a few people listened and learned. Only a
few remembered, but they turned out to be very im-

portant people when Mitchell's predicted war spread over both the Atlantic and Pacific. These men were "Hap" Arnold, "Tooey" Spaatz, Jimmy Doolittle, Joe McNarney, Ira Eaker, Lewis Brereton and Delos Emmons. They kept alive the spirit of Billy Mitchell and instilled it into the pilots they commanded and trained; the younger men who were to fly the Forts and Liberators, the Thunderbolts and Mustangs; and later on the "fire-can Jockeys" who were to tool Sabre jets over Korea.

Ignored, betrayed, belittled and downgraded, Billy Mitchell had started something that the politicians and bureaucrats could not halt.

The job had to be done, although Billy Mitchell did not live to see it. The years, the strain and the toil began to tell. He was fifty-five years old and the pace he had lived was beginning to show.

On a day when he had planned to go out for a ride, he suddenly decided to forego the pleasure. He tossed his gloves and cap on the table, sat down before a winter fire, and said, "I'm tired. Do you think I'm growing old?"

His wife smiled, glad to see that at last he was acting sensibly. But to be safe, she called a doctor.

When the doctor arrived he reminded Mitchell, "You're no longer twenty years of age, you know. You are living just as you did in those days. You ride or hunt or fish all day, and I'm told you're always the life of the party and dance all hours of the night. You've got to take it easy."

Billy sighed at the thought, and resignedly gave up flying. He eased up in other ways and took the time to write a book based on the life of his old friend General Greely, who died that year, 1935. In this book he told of the general's famous Arctic adventures, and the task kept him quietly occupied for some months. On its completion he again yearned for the outdoors, the fields, streams and stables. Young Billy had to learn to ride and to know how to handle a rifle.

The power to drive himself and intensify the fight for a unified air force began to wane, but Mitchell still gave it as much as he could, when he should have been spending more time resting. Had he relaxed and been satisfied with what he had finally accomplished, he might have lived for many more years. But he was not content to simply fade away like the proverbial old soldier. He obviously wished to die with his boots on; to go out in a blaze of glory.

His first serious heart attack occurred on January 28, 1936, and his doctor sent him off to Doctors' Hospital in New York. There they managed to keep him quiet for about three weeks. But he was always restless and his mind seethed with new ideas, new topics to write about, new views to present to someone in authority. He never gave himself a chance. On February 19, 1936, Billy Mitchell passed away.

He could have been buried in Arlington Cemetery with many other hero pilots of his day, but he chose instead to have his family take him back to Wisconsin, the home of the Mitchells. In the dead of winter his body was buried in Milwaukee, where, in the unforgettable spring of 1898, he had enlisted as a youth to go off to war. There was no military escort, but an American Legion Post party fired a salute and sounded Taps. No monument stands over the grave. It needs none. Billy Mitchell left the foundation of today's United States Air Force to mark his memory.

Although they came belatedly, honors were to be his. Eleven years after his death Congress passed a special bill promoting him, retroactively to the date of his death, to the rank of Major General.

BIBLIOGRAPHY

Burlingame, Roger, *General Billy Mitchell*. McGraw-Hill Book Co., Inc., 1952

Gavreau, Emile H., *The Wild Blue Yonder*. E. P. Dutton & Co., Inc., 1944

Gavreau, Emile H., and Cohen, Lester, *Billy Mitchell*. E. P. Dutton & Co., Inc., 1942

Levine, Isaac Don, *Mitchell, Pioneer of Air Power*. Duell, Sloan & Pearce, Inc., 1958

Mitchell, Ruth, *My Brother Bill*. Harcourt, Brace & Company, 1953

Mitchell, William, *General Greely*. G. P. Putnam's Sons, 1936

—— *Memoirs of World War I*. Random House, 1960

—— *Our Air Force*. E. P. Dutton & Co., Inc., 1921

—— *Skyways*. J. B. Lippincott Co., 1930

—— *Winged Defense*. G. P. Putnam's Sons, 1925

Pershing, John J., *My Experiences in the World War*. Frederick A. Stokes Company, 1931

Woodward, Helen, *General Billy Mitchell*. Duell, Sloan & Pearce, Inc., 1959

INDEX